Brian Fleming Research & Learning Library
Ministry of Education
Ministry of Training, Colleges & Universities
900 Bay St. 13th Floor, Mowat Block
Toronto, ON M7A 1L2

THE LIEUTENANT GOVERNOR OF ONTARIO
LA LIEUTENANTE GOUVERNEURE DE L'ONTARIO

Foreword

As Honorary Patron, I congratulate Family Day Care Services on 150 years of outstanding service to the children of Toronto. As social conditions and childcare practices have evolved, this agency has demonstrated unwavering commitment to meeting the changing needs of children in the best possible way.

On this anniversary, and in this volume, we salute the "Lady Managers" whose orphanage gave refuge to destitute children, the foster parents who opened their homes to those in need, and the childcare providers who deliver Toronto's primary day care services. All deserve our respect and gratitude.

On behalf of all Ontarians, I commend Family Day Care Services for the inspiring story told in these pages — a story of the generosity, dedication and service that improved, and sometimes saved, the lives of countless Toronto children.

Hilary M. Weston

For the Children

For the Children

150 Years of Caring
for Children and Families

Written by Bob Cooper

Photo essay by Larry Zacher

Family Day Care Services

Abbeyfield Publishers
Toronto, Ontario

Copyright © 2001 Family Day Care Services

All rights reserved. No portions of this book may be reproduced or transmitted in any form or by any means, electronic or mechanical, including photocopying, recording, scanning, e-mail, or any information storage or retrieval system.

Published in 2001 by Abbeyfield Publishers, a division of The Abbeyfield Companies Ltd.,
33 Springbank Avenue, Toronto Ontario Canada M1N 1G2

Ordering information:
Distributed in Canada by Hushion House Distributors Ltd
36 Northline Road Toronto Ontario Canada M4B 3E2

Canadian Cataloguing in Publication Data
Bob Cooper
    For the children

ISBN 1-894584-08-2
1. Child welfare – Ontario – Toronto Region – History. 2. Family social work – Ontario – Toronto Region – History. I. Title.

HV746.T6C66 2001   362.7'09713'541   C00-933020-8

Written by Robert Cooper
Photo essay by Larry Zacher
Edited by Bill Belfontaine
Cover and book design by Karen Petherick
Printing by TTP Tradeworx Ltd.

This book was published with the financial support of PricewaterhouseCoopers and Osler, Hoskin & Harcourt

---

The accuracy of the information contained on the following pages is based according to research documents supplied by Family Day Care Services, with the exceptions of the vignettes which are strictly the fictional creations of the author. Should there be errors or omissions of relevant nature to the story please advise Family Day Care Services in writing.

Every effort has been made to contact the estate of Norman Hornyansky for permission regarding his artwork of St. James Cathedral and St. Lawrence Hall. The copy of the artwork used in this book was obtained from the City of Toronto Art Collection.

Dedication

I dedicate this book to the children past and present, to the memory of the Lady Managers, and to the donors and volunteers who, for 150 years, have given without stint their time, talent and money to one of Canada's most venerable institutions.

Bob Cooper
Fergus, Ontario
January 1, 2001

150 Years of Caring for Children and Families

This original stained glass fixture is on display in Family Day Care Services' head office.
The reference to 1849 is unexplained in any of the existing historical documents.
The Orphans' Home and Female Aid Society was incorporated on August 2, 1851.

Table of Contents

150 Years of Caring for Children and Families

Acknowledgements	xiii
From the Author	xv
From the Publisher	xvii
The Orphans' Home 1851 – 1926	1
Protestant Children's Homes 1926 – 1971	69
Family Day Care Services 1971 – 2001	121
For the Children … and their future	161
Photo Album	169
Photo Credits	179

Acknowledgements

I am sincerely grateful to the following people for the help they gave me during the research and writing stages of this project.

Family Day Care Services staff members Anne Bird, Liz Colley, Maria de Wit, Bev O'Connell, Lisa Pecarski, Jill Poisson, Cheryl Rogers, Janet Tipton and Jean Wise; Dorothy Duncan, Ontario Historical Society; Carl Benn for his writings on The Yonge Street Rebellion; Rae B. Fleming for *From Horses to Stage Coaches, Street Cars, Jitneys, and Subways: Two Hundred Years of Transportation on the Longest Street in the World*; Jeanne Hopkins, who wrote *The Road is Open! Travel, Tollgates, and Hotels on Yonge Street*; Stephen A. Speisman, Ontario Jewish Archives and author of *The Jews of Toronto*, and of *Munificent Parsons* and *Municipal Parsimony*; Major David Pitcher, Salvation Army; Melany Persaud, Children's Aid Society of Toronto; Suzanne Lout, Archives of the Roman Catholic Diocese of Toronto; Linda Wicks, Archives of the Sisters of Saint Joseph; Mary Rae Shank, Toronto Public Reference Library, Baldwin Room; Lorraine Auburn, Chara Kirkman and Gwyneth Cunningham, Black Creek Pioneer Village; Karen Wagner, Wellington County Museum and Archives; Deanna Stevens, Wellington County Library, Centre Wellington Branch; Alvin Koop, Children's Aid Society of Guelph and Wellington County; Linda Pearson, my (much cleverer) sister, for proofreading parts of the manuscript; Cassandra Wong and Angelo Sgabellone, University Settlement; Irene L. Kyle, M.Sc., Ph.D.; Martha Friendly, Centre for Urban and Community Studies, University of Toronto; Simeonie Kunnuk, Inuit Tapirisat of Canada; Judy Nicholson-Flow, Joan Aaron and Rev. Carol Nash-Lowden formerly of Protestant Children's Homes; Bev Leaver and Cathie Leard of Jessie's; Mark Cuddy, City of Toronto Archives.

From the Author

I wish to thank the Board of Family Day, in particular Liz Howson, John Fauquier and Bob Hollingshead, and Family Day Executive Director, Maria de Wit, for giving me the opportunity to write this book.

I also wish to thank my good friend and co-labourer on this project, Larry Zacher, who, despite the numerous other duties he performs for Family Day, still found the time to roll up his sleeves and pitch in with the research and to offer valuable insights and timely advice. He was especially helpful in seeking out and assembling the many pictures that form what amounts to a photo essay, which parallels the narrative account of Family Day's 150-year history.

My debt to Dr. Irene Kyle is immeasurable. She gave unselfishly of her time to ensure that the story of child care in Ontario was accurately reflected in the narrative. Despite a busy schedule that included writing her own manuscript, Irene still found time to make corrections and improvements to mine – and she did it all with great patience and grace.

Book designer, Karen Petherick has done her usual exemplary job of presenting words and pictures in a way that is calculated to evoke the greatest emotional impact in the reader while, at the same time, allowing the information to flow naturally and unhindered.

And finally, Bill Belfontaine, who heads up Abbeyfield Publishers, has, once again, published a book that casts light on a little-known part of Canada's history, thereby permitting Canadians to see themselves in ways few have seen themselves before.

From the Publisher

One hundred and fifty years of service! A substantial achievement by dedicated volunteers and staff over the decades that constantly drew on inadequate resources to make a home for orphans and children seeking shelter for any one of a hundred reasons.

"For the Children" will fascinate you, as it did me when I was called to bring together the group of dedicated professionals who so capably tell and illustrate the suffering and heartache that turned, through loving care, into children's smiles of belonging.

Toronto cannot call itself a world-class city today because of bricks and mortar alone. No, it takes a community with soul, starting with the heartbeats of the handful of women and men who often struggled through mud-filled streets and community degradation to bring a child to safety.

Their pioneer social concern continues today, characterized by glowing computers in the bright millennium of our new century. Yet, the need has not changed; children become hurt, they crave love and care so the need is no less worthwhile than what was started a century and a half ago.

If a salute is to be awarded to the people of Toronto, it must first be directed at the hundreds of volunteers, staff and donors who have given life to a child when all others failed.

Am I proud, in my small effort at publishing this book, to be associated with this company of people down through the years? Yes, a hundred times, yes. And to my associates Bob Cooper, writer; Larry Zacher, photograph essayist; Karen Petherick, book designer; Christopher Kott, book printing and binding, may I thank them for a job very well done.

V. Wm. (Bill) Belfontaine

150 Years of Caring for Children and Families

The Orphans' Home

1851–1926

TORONTO, CANADA WEST.
From the top of the Jail

Toronto 1850

The dazzling autumn sunrise set the surface of the lake ablaze. From his nest in the hayloft, Tom shielded his eyes and squinted down upon the broad, dusty back of the dray horse, whose stable he had secretly shared the past few nights. Twin plumes of breath from the horse's nostrils told Tom there had been another frost, the second one this week and it was only mid-September. He rubbed his bare feet together in a vain attempt to restore feeling. After several seconds there was still no sensation, so he drew his knees up to his chest and began to knead his feet vigorously. When feeling at last returned, it brought searing pain, which drew tears and soon gave way to the fierce itch of chilblains that no amount of scratching would ease.

The boy cursed himself – in so far as a ten-year-old innocent, abandoned by a drunken brawler of a father whose wife had run off, is capable of cursing himself – for having been too proud to have accepted the battered but stout pair of brogan boots offered to him two days before by a farmer's wife. The woman and her husband had seen him prowling barefoot down by the wharves at the foot of Yonge Street when they had brought their wagon into town to deliver produce to market.

It was not the first time the couple had noticed the boy. He'd kept to himself, never associating with the dozens of other wharf rats and waifs who wandered the waterfront and streets of Toronto – many of them the orphans of Famine Irish immigrants who'd come to the Canadas in the late 1840s. Neither was it the first time Tom had noticed them. But they'd never been accompanied by children. Perhaps, thought Tom, they had none.

On this particular day, the woman had nudged her husband's elbow and spoken a furtive word in his ear. He had responded immediately by bringing his team to a halt. She had climbed down from the wagon and, smiling encouragingly at Tom, who stood several yards away, held out the rough, hobnailed boots to him.

"These is for you, boy," she had called. "Mister Sykes and me thinks it an awful sin you haven't any boots."

150 Years of Caring for Children and Families

"Don't need none, missus," Tom had lied, before scrambling on top of a long row of barrels and pretending to give his full attention to a steamboat easing into the wharf.

He had chanced a quick glance over his shoulder in time to see the motherly look of concern on her face. In lieu of the boots, she had set two apples on the rough wooden planking of the wharf, before climbing back onto the wagon beside her husband. When they had driven a safe distance away, Tom had jumped down, run to the apples and snatched them up. He had devoured one immediately and tucked the other inside his tattered, homespun shirt. He would eat it later that day with an egg he would find in the hayloft. Raw eggs made him retch, but at least they could still the pangs of hunger that constantly gnawed at his stomach.

Now, Tom longed for those boots on this frosty morning as he rolled out of his nest in the hay and slid noiselessly to the ground, taking care to avoid startling a hen roosting a few feet away. If he accidentally set her to squawking, he might alert the drayman who owned the horse and stable and lived with his wife and four small children in a clapboard house not thirty feet away. As a trespasser, Tom would most certainly be in for a beating, if he were caught.

On tiptoe, to avoid detection and to preserve what little warmth he'd managed to coax back into his feet, he picked his way through the muck and manure until he stood shivering beside the gatepost in the shadow of the horse. Carefully, he reached through the fence, lifted the lid on a bin that stood beside the gate and scooped out a handful of oats, which he held up to the horse. When his small hand was clean, the boy scratched the animal's soft muzzle then scooped up another handful, which he stuffed into his mouth. Bits and pieces of the coarse grain caught in his throat and he had to stifle the urge to hack and cough. A third handful went into one of the pockets of his coarse woollen trousers. From another pocket he withdrew a fat carrot that he'd pilfered from someone's backyard garden the day before. He snapped it in two, offered half to the horse, and began to nibble on the other half. It was not much of a breakfast, but it was all he had. He might find better pickings at the market later that morning, but he'd have to be careful, for the boys who ran errands for the merchants

Family Day Care Services

kept a sharp eye out for strays like Tom. If they caught him, they wouldn't hesitate to fetch him a kick before handing him over to the constable. And that would most certainly mean jail, where he could expect to be locked up with petty thieves, drunkards and hardened criminals.

Mid-morning found Tom loitering about the bustling market on King Street, near City Hall. Though the morning sun had burned off the frost, there was still a bite to the air and shivers seized the boy.

Just inside the open door of the market someone had placed a tin pie plate containing cow's milk straight from the udder. Stray cats that haunted the market were eagerly fighting over it. It had been many weeks since Tom had tasted milk. His rumbling stomach got the better of him. Ignoring the grit and bits of straw that the wind and careless feet had kicked into it, the boy dropped to his knees and, scattering the cats, picked up the plate and began to guzzle.

Noblesse Oblige

There have always been two Torontos, one for the haves and another for the have-nots. The story of Family Day Care Services begins when young Tom roamed the streets and the wharves of mid-nineteenth century Toronto. Owing to the benevolence of the women representing some of the city's leading families and churches, the two Torontos met, changing forever the lives of some of the city's poorest children, many of them orphans.

To understand the lasting importance of that encounter, it is first necessary to place it in its proper historical context. For the first half of the nineteenth century, Toronto lagged behind Kingston, Montreal and Quebec as a commercial centre. A depression had occurred in 1837. By the 1850s, however, Toronto was coming into its own. The economy of Ontario – that portion of upper Canada occupying the land adjacent to the easternmost Great Lakes – began to shift from primarily agricultural to industrial capitalism. People drifted away from farming communities to the United States, the Canadian West, or to Ontario's larger towns and cities. Many came to Toronto and swelled the ranks of the labour force. Despite another depression in 1857, the 1850s were a decade of rapid urbanization and industrial growth during which textile mills, metalworking, farm implement and machinery factories sprang up around the city. Toronto's economy boomed and it became a transportation and manufacturing hub. Many of the city's ninety streets were macadamized, downtown was gaslit, and King Street, a main thoroughfare, was planked for two miles. There was even a rudimentary network of wooden water mains in some sections of the city.

But not all of the city's thirty thousand inhabitants shared in the prosperity. Thousands were doomed to live in poverty, the seeds of their misery having been sewn years before and far away, on the other side of the Atlantic. Over the course of the next few decades,

150 Years of Caring for Children and Families

the sweatshop system would dominate industrial Toronto and compel legions of working-class men, women and children to toil for mere pennies a day in poorly ventilated, inadequately heated and gloomily lit lofts and cellars.

Between 1832 and 1835, successive waves of English and Irish immigrants sailed to Canada. Most of them were desperately poor and illiterate, the victims of crop failures and economic recession. Cholera and typhus decimated their ranks. Those who did not die aboard ship were quarantined at Grosse Ile, situated in the St. Lawrence River, 25 miles downstream from Quebec City. During those years, the quarantine station examined more than 100,000 immigrants for disease.

Ten years later, in 1845, reports of a potato disease in Ireland began to circulate. The following year, the potato crop failed again, resulting in famine and yet another outbreak of cholera and typhus. Hardest hit were the cottiers – peasants who farmed less than an acre of rented land. In the years to follow, between one and a half and two million were driven out of Ireland by their English landowners. More than half a million Irish immigrants were exiled, starving, sick and penniless, to British North America. And while a large proportion of them moved to the United States, many stayed in Canada. Like their kinsmen who had come before them, and like the tens of thousands of impoverished English immigrants from the slums of Liverpool and London, they were crammed like cordwood below decks aboard leaky, rat-infested boats that were rife with disease and which came to be known alternately as the "fever fleet" and the "typhus ships." Tens of thousands of these miserable folk – enough to populate a small city – never completed the crossing; they died en route. A few words were said over their fetid bodies before they were dumped overboard into the cold, black waters of the North Atlantic. Most vulnerable on these sad journeys of several weeks were the very young and the very old. The majority of those who survived settled in either Montreal or Toronto, providing cheap labour willing to work for starvation wages, and thereby helping to fuel the economic expansion of both cities over the next two decades.

By 1851, the population of Upper Canada approached one million. Most immigrants came from the British Isles. Roughly 20 percent were English and 20 percent Scottish. Though many had lived as paupers in the old country, a significant number were farmers and skilled craftsmen of one kind or another. Among them were ex-military officers, professional people, successful merchants, school teachers, and clergymen. The latter represented Britain's desire to reproduce the English class system in North America. They would compose the political elite of Canada. The overwhelming majority of the remaining 60 percent of immigrants were Irish. Within 25 years, they would become the largest ethnic community in every Canadian town and city outside Quebec.

The "Famine Irish" who came to Toronto in the late 1840s and early 1850s in search of a new life were hated. There was a severe shortage of adequate housing. The situation worsened when, in 1849, a fire destroyed St. James Cathedral and a number of surrounding dwelling houses. Of course, the influx of more immigrants placed an additional strain on critically low housing stocks. Feelings toward the newcomers hardened even more when outbreaks of typhus and cholera occurred in 1849, claiming the lives of more than 500 people. They were stigmatized as unclean and illiterate and forced to live in slums. Life for them in their adopted city was hardly better than it had been back home. Confined to the rougher precincts of the city, they were forced to rub shoulders with, and all too often join the ranks of beggars, prostitutes, drunks, and street gangs. Frequently, they came to the attention of the police. When they sought employment or lodging they met with hostility. Signs read "No Irish Need Apply" and "No Irish or Dogs." And it didn't matter whether the Irishman was Roman Catholic or Protestant – "Mick" or Orangeman, as they were labelled – the prevailing attitude harboured by the majority of the English and Scots was that all Irishmen were the same – no good!

St. James Cathedral.

"Taught by that power which pities me, I learn to pity them."

ORPHAN'S HOME AND FEMALE AID SOCIETY,

Under the Patronage of Her Excellency the Countess of Elgin and Kincardine.

Original Prospectus drafted June, 1851

A PERMANENT ASYLUM for the relief of ORPHANS in Upper Canada, based on principles of pure philanthropy, cannot fail to merit the patronage of a liberal and discerning Public.

The sufferings of the most helpless of their sex, the *Female Orphans* especially, must interest the sympathies of the Ladies of Toronto; it is therefore proposed to establish in this City an *"Orphan's Home"* and to unite therewith a *"Female Aid Society"*—the whole to be under the exclusive management of Ladies.

With regard to the *Orphan's Home*—the establishment will be Protestant—there being already a Roman Catholic Asylum, and although it is impossible to ascertain the *exact* number of Protestant Orphans who are objects of charity, the number must be considerable, as the Roman Catholics have seldom less than 40 and at one time had upwards of 50 orphans of their persuasion under their proper care. The Orphan's Home now to be established will be open to the whole county of York, and the orphans will be fed, clothed and instructed, up to the age of 12 or 14 years, when they will be apprenticed to respectable persons.

With regard to the *Female Aid Society*—it is grounded on the principle that "prevention is better than cure," for there is little doubt that poverty and destitution are the precursors of immorality and crime—Numbers of young and innocent Females are annually driven from the path of uprightness and purity, into the vortex of iniquity and irrecoverable degradation, in consequence of being unable to procure *immediate* employment either as Seamstresses or Servants—In the city of Toronto alone during the year 1850, out of 1608 apprehensions for crime, 499 were females, who if they had had a place of refuge instead of being a disgrace to themselves and a burden upon the Public, might have become useful Members of Society.—Of course *great care* will be taken in this Institution, to select such Females only as are properly recommended, who, during their stay in the house, will be placed under the influence of Christian privileges and instruction, independently of having a comfortable home, and possessing the advantage of the kind and judicious counsel of the Ladies Committee.—A registry of the inmates will be kept to enable Families to obtain domestic servants.

The Ladies of Montreal and Quebec have set a noble example—In the former City, lately was held the 29th Anniversary of *their* Protestant Orphan Asylum, and the annual Report then read, fully proves the great and numerous benefits which that Association have bestowed.—Their report concludes with the following impressive remarks, "And now to the care of that Beneficent Providence, who has so eminently blessed the exer-"tions of those who have undertaken to supply the Spiritual and Temporal wants of the orphan, the Directresses "confidently commit the future welfare of their charge, praying that *He* who has vouchsafed to say 'That who-"soever shall receive one of such children in *His* name receiveth *Him*,' will be graciously pleased to inspire "the hearts of the faithful, 'That they be rich in good works and ready to distribute, laying up in store a good "foundation against the time to come.' "—The total number of orphans benefitted in Montreal during the year 1850 amounted to 45.

The Ladies of Quebec, also, have recently celebrated the 22nd anniversary of *their* Female Orphan Asylum—The neat, healthy and happy appearance of the Children, who were present to the number of 26, was an evidence of the care and kindness bestowed upon them, and was an ample testimony of the persevering zeal of the Ladies of their committee, as well as of the conscientious manner in which the Matron and Assistant discharged their duties.—The total number of orphans admitted since the foundation of that asylum, amounted to 116.

Is there not as wide a field for the charitable exertions of the Ladies of Toronto within their district, as the Ladies of Montreal and Quebec have found in their's? Beyond all doubt there is, and it is confidently hoped that the Ladies of Toronto will at once come forward to rescue their unfortunate fellow creatures from penury and misery.

"The Orphans' Home and Female Aid Society of Toronto" is proposed to be supported by the following means—

    1st—By the ordinary Annual Grant from the Legislature,—in amount the same as similar institutions in the Province.
    2nd—By voluntary subscriptions from Heads of Families—not exceeding one pound per annum each.
    3rd—By Donations and Legacies, and
    4th—By an Annual Musical Festival or Bazaar.

In addition to which, it is expected that residents in the Country Districts will contribute in the shape of produce &c.

Two Gentlemen have already generously given a valuable site for the buildings and grounds, in the neighbourhood of Saint George's Square, and plans for the Edifices have been gratuitously offered.; all that is required now is the organization necessary for raising the Funds, and settling the system of management.

Application will be made during the present Session of Parliament, for an Act of Incorporation, and when the Act is obtained, Her Excellency the Countess of Elgin and Kincardine has most kindly consented to become the Patroness of the Institution.

The first meeting for the formation of the Society will be held on Monday next, the 16th instant, at 3 o'clock P. M., in the Mechanics' Institute, Toronto. The Reverend Dr. Lett, (as clergyman of the locality in which the building is to be erected), has consented to be Chairman, and the support of the *Public generally* is most earnestly solicited, in order that this truly charitable work may be accomplished.

Should a personal attendance be inconvenient, a note expressive of approval of the charity, addressed to the Chairman of the meeting, may be posted, directed to Box 307 in the Post Office, which will enable the Committee to make their further arrangements without delay.

Toronto, 9th June 1851.

From 1851 to 1926 The Orphans' Home produced a poster-sized document each year, acknowledging the Officers, Patron(s), Lady Managers and other notable persons.

These documents are kept at Family Day Care Services' head office.

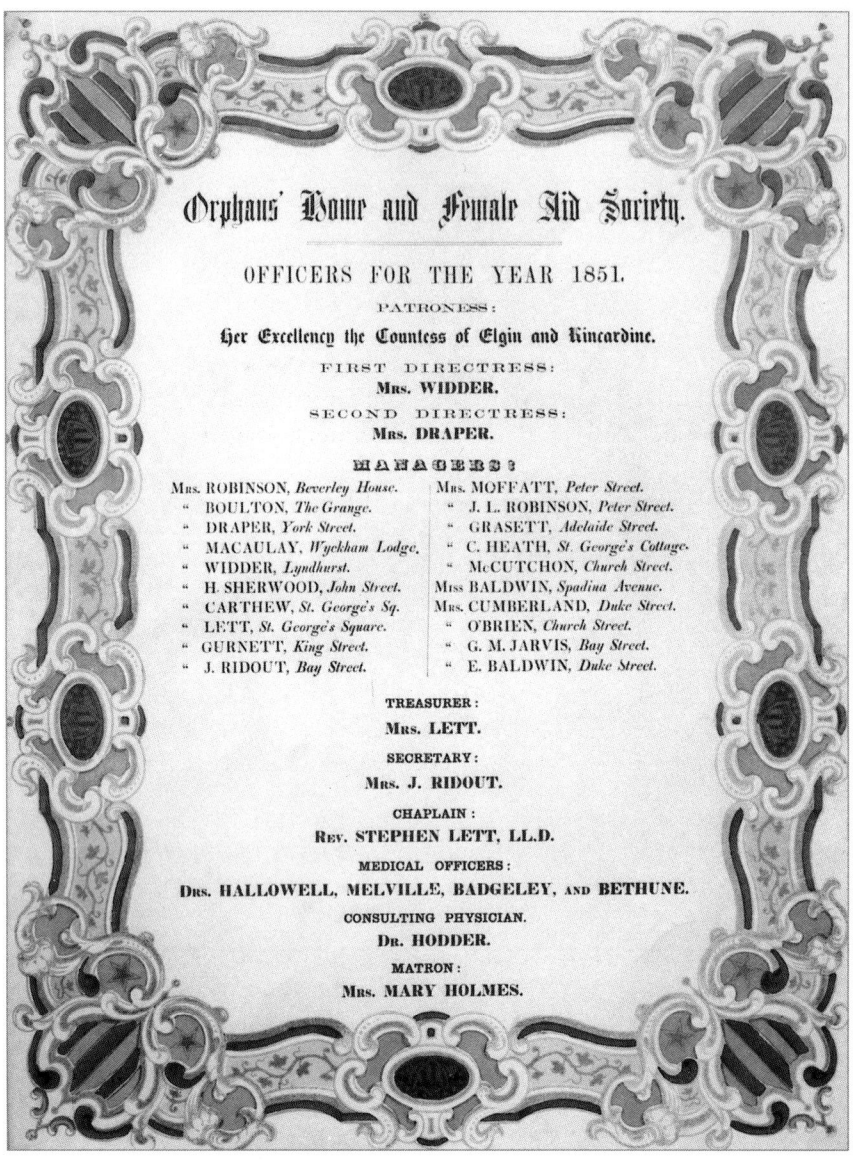

In 1850, in his annual report to the mayor and city council, Chief Constable George Allen, who kept statistics recording the country of origin of all offenders, provided an insight into the lives of Toronto's Irish community. Of the 1,612 people arrested that year for various offences, 1,048 were Irish men and women – 65 percent! In fact, more than twice as many Irish women were arrested that year than English men.

In an age when public hangings were commonplace, indeed were occasions for general amusement, even the lower end of the sentencing scale was harsh. In 1850, of the 435 people sent to jail for one to thirty days for minor offences, thirty of those locked up were children. Not until 1857, when the provincial government passed an Act to Provide Gaols for Young Offenders, were convicted "infants," children under twenty-one years of age, segregated from hardened criminals and housed in separate institutions.

Some influential members of the middle and upper classes believed it was their responsibility to rescue the poor. They were motivated primarily by religious convictions, as evidenced by the fact that virtually all relief efforts were associated with specific church congregations. They saw the endowment of social welfare purely as a function of the church and of benevolent societies that were established in the 1830s. Among them were the Saint George Society, which provided relief to the English poor and the Saint Andrew's Society, which cared for destitute Scottish immigrants. The Irish Protestant Benevolent Society was established in the 1870s for the same purpose. Churches and benevolent societies were aided further by organizations such as the Odd Fellows, the Orange Lodge, and the Sons of England, all of which contributed money for the relief of the poor.

In the 1840s and 1850s, impoverished black refugees from the United States, who had been spirited north by means of the Underground Railroad, received help from the Queen Victoria Benevolent Society, a group composed of women who attended a

Bishop Strachan
(Strachan, John 1778–1867)

number of local black churches. The Society received further aid from members of Toronto's Anti-Slavery Society and other influential Toronto families, who held benefit concerts to raise money.

Because voluntary organizations dispensed aid to the poor, all governments absolved themselves of virtually all responsibility. Only during times of severe economic hardship did it occur to upper class Victorian Toronto to lay some of the responsibility for the care of the poor at the feet of their elected representatives.

In a letter dated November 30, 1857, Bishop John Strachan urged Mayor Hutchison to consider instituting a small tax increase in order to generate funds with which to "strengthen and encourage" the relief efforts of the city's churches. Toronto, said Strachan, had become a haven for indigent people from all parts of the province. The ranks of the destitute had swollen to the point where voluntary welfare could no longer carry the load alone. But the government remained deaf to such pleas. Ultimately, it was the sense of noblesse oblige, which was felt by the upper class, and the overriding British imperialist determination to bring civilization to the colonies that led to the establishment of the city's first charities.

Nevertheless, the moral obligation and generosity of spirit felt by the haves did not extend to all of the have-nots – only to the young, the old, and the infirm; the "deserving poor," as they were regarded. All others, regardless of circumstances – economic depression, famine, and wholesale displacement, for example – were seen as the "undeserving poor." In the minds of so many who had attained a level of comfort and security in the young city, the onus for poverty rested exclusively on the shoulders of those who suffered it. The privileged classes believed slums were "immoral" and so were those who inhabited them. The undeserving poor got nothing more or less than they deserved.

Christian charity aside, a strong element of self-serving pragmatism was inherent in much of the social rescue work undertaken in Victorian Toronto. It was motivated by fear of the ever-growing pauper class, which, some believed, might rise up one day and overthrow the economic system that subjugated them. So it had to be admitted that some people were prodded to action more by a desire to maintain the status quo than they were by a desire to comply with the "great commandment" to love their neighbour as themselves. Better to be seen rendering help to a few than to risk the wrath of many and the possibility of revolution.

The depression of 1837 spawned even more beggars than already plied the streets of Toronto. It compelled the City to convert an old house on Richmond Street into a House of Industry, or workhouse, at which the "industrious poor" might give up begging and contribute to society – men by breaking rock for public roads, and women by knitting clothing for sale, the proceeds going to support the institution.

The House of Industry also took in neglected children. Many as newborns, were left in baskets provided for that purpose on the porch of the workhouse. Children lived at the House of Industry until they were old enough to be apprenticed. Most, however, were "boarded-out" to homes both in Toronto and throughout the surrounding rural areas.

Impoverished children were by far the worst off. Their lives were tragic and in many cases, brief. Their parents, if they were alive, seldom could afford to feed or clothe them. They were shunted from the home of one relative or friend to that of another, or delivered as unpaid servants to people occupying much higher rungs on the economic ladder. Often in such circumstances their masters mistreated them, and with impunity, because there did not yet exist any sort of formal supervision over such arrangements. Many children whose parents had died or were no longer capable or willing to care for them ended up on the street having to fend for themselves.

Cramped living conditions and poor sanitation permitted common childhood diseases like measles and whooping cough to claim the lives of untold numbers. It has been estimated that one in seven children born alive (there were many stillbirths) died within the first twelve months, and that of those who survived the first year, one in seven would not see their seventh birthday. Ill health and poor nutrition conspired to prevent working-class boys from reaching their full adult height until their mid-twenties.

Generally speaking, children were valued primarily for the work they did. They were a ready and inexpensive source of labour – an economic asset and nothing more. To reinforce this commonly held notion, the Orphans' Act of 1799 bound orphaned children to indentured lives – girls until they were 18 and boys until 21.

Yorkville 1850

Katherine draped the rug over the fence and began to flail it with the carpet-beater. With each blow, the beater raised a heart-shaped welt on the rug that turned her stomach. How she hated this weekly chore, for she had seen the same heart-shaped welts on her mother's thighs and back. Striking the rug with the same weapon that had injured the only person she had ever truly known and loved was almost more than the girl could bear. She let the carpet-beater fall from her hand and, sagging against the fence, dropped to the ground where she sat staring at the angry, red fissures on her fingertips. Though she was only 13 years old, Katherine already had the rough, raw hands and sallow complexion of a middle-aged charwoman. As had happened to her mother before her, days of drudgery begun in pre-dawn darkness that ended close to midnight, had already robbed Katherine of her childhood and now sucked the rest of her adolescence from her.

Since the age of six, Katherine had been in the service of the miller and his family. She'd been indentured to them the very day her mother had been shut away in the insane asylum, suffering from hysterics — or so the miller's wife had claimed.

Katherine's mother's name was Grace. As she sat hunkered against the fence, Katherine was appalled to realize that her mother had never in her entire life heard her own name uttered in the spirit of love or friendship. Katherine had naturally called her "mother." The miller and his wife had tarnished the beautiful name by turning it alternately into a command or an expletive.

"She's weak in the mind, your mother, and full of wild stories," the miller's wife had hissed the day Grace was taken away. "Don't know why it was we kept her so long, for she never earned her keep."

Though Katherine knew otherwise, she held her tongue for fear that the carpet beater might be used on her. There was no doubt that the miller's wife had worked poor Grace, first as a child and then as a woman, like a rented mule. Nor was there any doubt that the miller himself figured

The lives of impoverished children were tragic and in many cases, brief.

150 Years of Caring for Children and Families

prominently in her mother's misery. His cruel visits to the servant girl's room late at night, even in Katherine's presence, had contributed to a wretched state of mind that had driven Grace, at the age of 27, to try hanging herself from the lintel over the scullery. She had failed, and Katherine couldn't decide if that was merciful or not.

Angered by the inconvenience, the miller's wife had taken the cost of Grace's transport to the asylum out of her wages.

In 1851, the passage through Parliament of the Apprentices and Minors Act represented an early attempt to protect children from the exploitation many suffered at the hands of unscrupulous employers. The realization was widespread that large numbers of children were in serious need of protection from all manner of abuse and neglect. This coincided with the Victorian belief that moral rectitude could be inculcated in destitute children if they were afforded the opportunity to live in a clean, well-regulated environment.

Over the next 60 years, a large number of religiously affiliated organizations would set up asylums to rescue the waifs of the city.

In the spring of 1851, Doctor Rees, Captain Charles Jones and a businessman named Tynman, all of whom occupied offices in the vicinity of the post office on Toronto Street, became concerned by the presence of dozens of homeless children who played each day in the street beneath their windows. To be sure, these little "street Arabs," as they were then called, were a nuisance, a major source of annoyance. But they were also pitiable, and in need of protection.

Aside from their youth, these waifs had nothing in common with the children of the upper classes with whom the three gentlemen were acquainted. Shiny tin soldiers and ringletted dolls with crinolines were far beyond the reach of ragamuffins such as these. Their toy box was the street. For amusement, they had to make do with whatever they could scavenge – a discarded bottle or

Family Day Care Services

piece of cork, the broken spoke of a wagon wheel or a rusty barrel hoop. Their clothes, all hand me downs, hung in tattered layers upon their unwashed little bodies. Even the secondhand clothing worn by middle class children would have been often, but expertly, patched; frugality and skill with the needle being highly regarded virtues. But it had been a very long time since the rough woolen breeches and threadbare smocks worn by the street children had seen a needle and thread, for there was no one to do the mending. Nearly all of the waifs were barefoot, and even the hobnailed boots that a few were fortunate enough to have obtained were too badly worn or too poor a fit to provide comfort or protection.

Gangs of older boys were commonplace in mid-nineteenth century Toronto. For safety, the urchins ran in packs of half a dozen and more, following one or two leaders – the oldest, the toughest, or the most experienced, depending upon the brand of mischief being hatched or the tactic needed to acquire food, shelter, or to escape from danger. Their language was the coarse, often profane, vernacular of the drayman and the wharf rat. How could it have been otherwise? Many had no parents at all, but of those who did, perhaps a mother had been widowed and left destitute, or a father had found himself unable to raise a brood of children on his own, his wife having died, run off, or been caged up in the city's insane asylum. Left to their own devices, the waifs lived a catch-as-catch-can existence. They ate whatever their own craftiness and the occasional kind heart provided.

There were numerous reasons why these children had taken to the streets, but the overriding reason for their presence beneath the windows of Messrs. Rees, Jones, and Tynman, was the unremitting poverty imposed upon their class. Unless something were done to protect them, they might never survive it. The three men took the plight of the street children to Dr. Stephen Lett, Pastor of St. George's (Episcopalian) Church and to George Gurnett, Mayor of Toronto, who agreed that something had to be done.

Dr. Stephen Lett
Reverend Doctor Stephen Lett was determined to help Toronto's homeless children.

The Lady Managers

A few weeks after the three men brought the plight of the homeless children to the attention of Dr. Lett and Mr. Gurnett, a circular appeared in the city appealing to "the sympathies of the ladies of Toronto" to become involved in the establishment of a Protestant Orphans' Home and Female Aid Society, which would offer "relief and support to friendless orphans and destitute females" to whom would be given "religious and moral instruction." It would be run "under the exclusive management of ladies."

In part, the petition said:

"With regards to the Orphans' Home, the establishment will be Protestant, there being already a Roman Catholic Asylum and although it is impossible to ascertain the exact number of Protestant orphans who are objects of charity, the numbers must be considerable as the Roman Catholics have seldom less than forty, and at one time upwards of fifty orphans of their persuasion under proper care. The Orphans' Home now to be established will open to the whole county of York and the orphans will be fed, clothed and instructed up to the age of twelve or fourteen years when they will be apprenticed to respectable persons."

The circular announcing the Protestant Orphans' Home and Female Aid Society lauded the efforts of the women of Montreal who were celebrating their orphanage's twenty-sixth anniversary. And it set before the women of Toronto a challenge:

"Is there not as wide a field for the charitable exertions of the ladies of Toronto within their districts as the ladies of Montreal and Quebec have found in theirs? It is consistently hoped that the ladies of Toronto will at once come all forward to rescue their unfortunate fellow creatures from penury."

The new Society's motto would be, "Taught by the power that pities me, I learn to pity them." In the minds of the authors of the circular, the souls of those unfortunate people who lived in penury were in peril:

Family Day Care Services

"*...for there is little doubt,*" the circular went on to say, "*that poverty and destitution are the great precursors of immorality and crime.*"

The women hoped to ensure the financial viability of their enterprise by applying for an annual operating grant from the legislature of Ontario. They would charge the parents of children brought into care a modest and voluntary annual subscription fee of not more than one pound per year. Donations and legacies would of course be encouraged, as would gifts of farm produce. The ladies would also conduct fund-raising events like bazaars and musical festivals.

Though the names of the Honorable William Cayley and the Honorable Robert Baldwin, the Reform leader and supporter of responsible government in Canada, did not appear in the circular, it was announced that two men had made an offer of land on which an orphanage could be built, and that architectural plans had also been offered free of charge. An application would be made to Parliament for an Act of Incorporation. On the expectation that the charter would be granted, Her Excellency the Countess of Elgin and Kincardine had consented to become the first Patroness of the institution.

A public meeting was called for the afternoon of Saturday, June 14, 1851 at the Mechanics Institute of Toronto, which, like the Institutes in other Canadian cities, was the forerunner of the public library system. Because the proposed orphanage would be built in his parish, the Reverend Dr. Lett was asked to chair the meeting. It was well attended, and of the forty-nine nominees to the board of the Protestant Orphans' Home and Female Aid Society, thirty were elected. Control of the new institution was granted to "the ladies of the city." They would come to be known over the long history of the Society as "the lady managers." While the ladies assumed the responsibility of the day-to-day running of the Home, the gentlemen who joined them in an advisory capacity, as members of a Committee of Council, many of whom were their husbands or fathers, took charge of all financial and legal matters relating to the institution.

Mrs. McCaul
One of the Founders of this Institution
Rested from Her Labours July 1, 1896.

Decades before Canadian women won the right to vote or hold public office, and in an era when men believed their womenfolk ought to be spared exposure to both the underside of society and the rigours of running any enterprise, let alone an asylum for dependent children, the Act of Incorporation gave the Lady Managers full authority to conduct the affairs of the orphanage independent of their husbands. The Protestant Orphans' Home was among the few charitable organizations of the period that did not follow the rule of male administration. The wives and daughters of "old money" Tories, representing the Family Compact, and those of "new money" reformers, representing Toronto's burgeoning mercantile and middle class, sat on the original board of the Protestant Orphans' Home and Female Aid Society. The first register of the Society's Committee of Council and the roster of Lady Managers bore some of the most prominent names of the era: Robinson, Boulton, Widder, Gurnett, Ridout, Baldwin, Cumberland, and Jarvis.

The likelihood of acquiring donated land in the near future, a board composed of members of some of the most influential families in Toronto, and the patronage of the Countess of Elgin and Kincardine, assured the Society of a successful inauguration. All that remained for the enterprise to become a reality was to raise the money required to construct a proper building.

The Society's fund-raising campaign received a welcomed boost in October of 1851 when soprano Jenny Lind, who was billed as the Swedish Nightingale, staged a series of three concerts in Toronto. She devoted the proceeds of her final performance to charity. The money was turned over to the city clerk who identified a number of charitable organizations amongst which it might be divided. He advised Dr. Lett that the fledgling Society would receive two hundred pounds if its supporters raised an equal amount. The money from the Jenny Lind concert was turned over when, after only a few hours, Dr. Lett had succeeded in doing just that. The donation represented Toronto's first matching grant.

Cornerstone for the Sullivan Street Orphanage.

Family Day Care Services

FIRST APPEARANCE OF JENNY LIND IN AMERICA,
At Castle Garden Sept. 11th 1850.

Jenny Lind's first concert in America.

Proceeds from one of Jenny Lind's 1851 Toronto concerts were divided amongst several Toronto charities, including the Protestant Orphans' Home and Female Aid Society. It became the city's first matching grant.

Toronto, October 21, 1851

William's hand trembled as he held out his ticket to the usher. He had never before been to the St. Lawrence Hall, never been amongst so many finely dressed people, and never in his life felt so ashamed of his coarse woolen suit and thick-soled boots. But no matter, for he would gladly endure the disdainful stares of those around him for the chance to hear Mademoiselle Jenny Lind, the greatest soprano of the age. It was for this once in a lifetime opportunity that William had saved up enough money for two nights' stay in one of the city's humbler hostelries and coach fare from Port Credit, where he scratched out a meagre living teaching school in rented rooms near the harbour.

His hopes had nearly been dashed the day before the concert, for when he had gone to Nordheimer's music store on King Street to purchase his ticket he was met by a mob. Everyone was clambering for tickets, including a number of rough looking characters who were purchasing large numbers of them for later re-sale at inflated prices in front of the Hall. Push eventually came to shove and of course a few bloody noses. The police had to be called out and the front door of the store barricaded. William had been lucky enough to have purchased one of the few remaining tickets. It had cost him four dollars, the equivalent of several days' wages. But it was worth it.

Now in the dimly lit hall his heart raced as he waited to be captivated by the angelic voice that had conquered all of Europe and would, before the evening ended, own every heart in Toronto.

First, however, the preliminaries would have to be endured – a fantasia by clarinetist Signor Belletti, then an aria by tenor Signor Salvi, and finally something from Handel's Messiah played by violinist Joseph Burke. These performances proved adequate and each was followed by restrained applause. William was clearly not the only member of the audience of several hundred people impatient to see and hear the famous soprano.

Family Day Care Services

Enough! He hadn't come all this way, nor spent every last penny, to feign pleasure in this lot of buskers.

Then there was a brief moment of silence followed by tumultuous applause as there glided onto the stage a breathtakingly beautiful woman with long dark braided hair, and an oval face of such utter perfection that William's heart ached. She wore the costume of a peasant girl, which revealed ivory shoulders and a long graceful neck that required no adornment. She carried a nosegay which she held for an instant to smiling lips before curtsying demurely – first to the audience and then to her conductor and accompanist, Mr. Otto Goldschmidt.

Poor William was instantly stricken; Mademoiselle Lind could take his heart and do with it what she wished. Mercifully, he did not know that she and Goldschmidt were lovers, and that the following year, they would wed in Boston.

When the applause subsided, Goldschmidt bent to the keyboard, playing the opening chords of a fantasia by Thalberg. The Swedish Nightingale cupped her lovely hands beneath her breast and, gazing up at some unseen heaven, began to sing. In that instant, William knew that no sound he had ever heard, or would hear in the future, could approach the ineffable beauty of Jenny Lind's voice.

There followed arias by Bellini and Donizetti, and another fantasia by Belletti. She even sang Scottish standards like "John Anderson My Jo" and "Comin' Through the Rye." Occasionally, to allow the diva to rest, there were brief musical interruptions by Messrs. Salvi and Burke, which the crowd barely tolerated.

All too soon, the concert came to an end. Mademoiselle Lind retired from the stage amid cheers and shouts of "Bravo!" Slowly, William rose to his feet and shuffled to the exit. Outside the Hall, he made his way along King Street in the direction of his dowdy hotel, his heart in tatters. He couldn't have been happier.

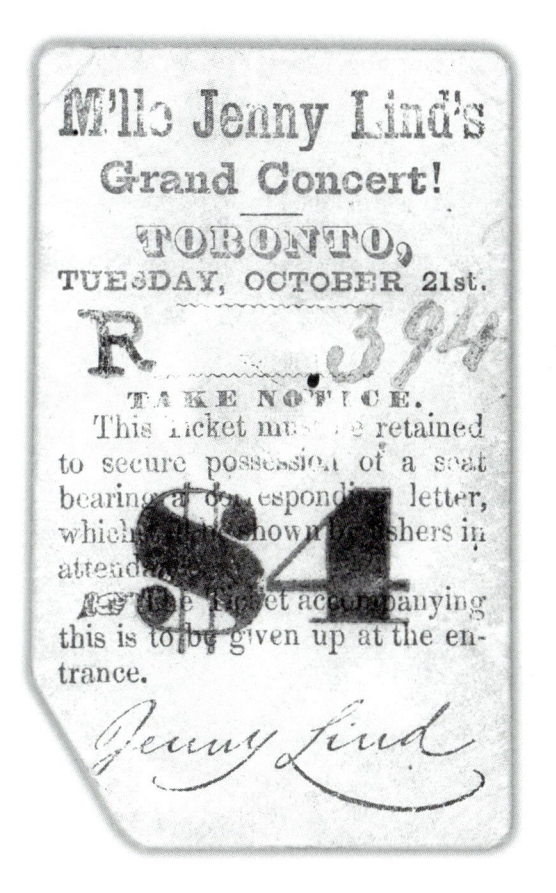

Robert Baldwin (1804–1858)
Parliamentary reformer, Robert Baldwin, was among those whose generosity made it possible for the Protestant Orphans' Home and Female Aid Society to serve Toronto's impoverished children.

The capital campaign was conducted over many months. While it proceeded, a small wooden house on the east side of Bay Street a few doors south of King Street was rented and used as an orphanage. It is not certain exactly when this happened, or even which of two buildings on Bay Street served as the Society's first orphanage. Either the house at 53 Bay Street, owned by Rev. Dr. James Richardson, or a house owned by Alexander Rennie at 45 Bay Street, may have been the actual location. An 1882 newspaper article mentioned the Richardson building and the Rennie building was referred to in the report of the Society sub-committee that was appointed to rent a house in 1853. In any event, until such time as the Society was able to build a permanent shelter of its own, there is some evidence to suggest that they used one of the buildings on Bay Street as an orphanage until 1854.

There is also reason to believe that the orphanage may have existed at one of the two Bay Street locations as early as the mid-1840s. Nearly 40 years later, at the official opening of the Society's orphanage on Dovercourt Road, a man by the name of Bennet, who was the Orange Grand Master for Ontario West, would recall that his organization had given financial assistance to the orphanage as early as 1844 or '45.

By 1852, the question of land remained unsettled. In July of the previous year, Messrs. Cayley and Baldwin had written to the Society to offer approximately half an acre of land east of Spadina Avenue near St. George's Square as long as "a permanent and respectable building is erected and the land enclosed." The following May, Mr. Baldwin wrote again to say that he and Cayley would withhold the deed for the land until such time as the building was erected, and that their offer had a two-year time limit on it. Baldwin was concerned that the land be used for an orphanage, not, as he apparently feared, as a profitable investment for the Society.

Also being considered as a potential site for the orphanage was a parcel of land nearer the lake at Victoria Square. But the acquisition of this land proved to be somewhat controversial.

When, in August 1852, a patent was issued granting the Society an acre of the Victoria Square tract, a man named Daly, who was in possession of it, refused to surrender it. The Society brought an action of ejectment against Daly, who threatened to seek an injunction in Chancery, as well as other unspecified legal proceedings.

Some members of the Society were concerned that a public legal battle might do their cause harm by alienating certain influential people in the city. Moreover, some families residing close to Victoria Square objected to the erection of an orphanage nearby. They didn't want an orphanage in their backyard. Accordingly, the Society abandoned its claim to the Victoria Square plot in exchange for land elsewhere. Two one-acre lots on Queen Street East, a lot near the Bathurst Barracks, and a four-acre parcel situated on the military reserve between the lunatic asylum and a brewery were all considered and, in their turn, rejected.

Jenny Lind even added her voice to the controversy, but this time less sweetly, in the form of a letter complaining that the erection of a building was taking too long. At last, an orphanage designed by Toronto architect John Harper was erected at a cost of 1,882 pounds on the land originally offered by Baldwin and Cayley. It was situated two blocks south of Dundas Street, east of Spadina, on the north side of Sullivan Street at number 12 (later listed on the city map as number 20). It was a three-storey, brick building that could accommodate up to 30 children. The Society would use the Sullivan Street building for the next 30 years, adding a west wing in 1860 and an east wing in 1864. The building incorporated an external staircase and infirmary. In honour of their major benefactors, the west wing became known as the Clergymen's Wing, and the east wing became known as the Orange Wing.

Sullivan St. Orphans' Home
When it opened in 1852, the Sullivan Street Home housed 30 children.

House of Providence

Built on Power Street in 1857, the House of Providence, which was run by the Roman Catholic Church, assisted so many Orange Irish that it came to be known affectionately as the House of Protestants.

The Quality of Mercy

Between the mid-nineteenth century and the end of the First World War, a dozen other child protection agencies were established throughout Toronto. They would share in the work being done by the Protestant Orphans' Home and Female Aid Society. For the most part, they would do so with minimal assistance from the government.

The Roman Catholic Orphans' Asylum of St. Paul's

One of the earliest of these was the orphans' asylum run by lay women of the parish of St. Paul's. In 1826, St. Paul's became the first Roman Catholic Church built in Toronto. It was situated on Power Street in Cabbagetown – then a mostly Irish quarter of the city immediately west of the Don River. The cash-strapped church received timely and generous financial help from a number of sources, including certain prominent Protestants of the day, such as Robert Baldwin and Samuel Jarvis, two men whose families would figure significantly in the story of nineteenth century orphanages.

Though the actual year is unknown, sometime prior to 1851, the wife of the Honourable John Elmsley, former Chief Justice of Upper Canada, and other women from the congregation of St. Paul's, had set up an orphanage on the west side of Nelson Street – later called Jarvis Street – between Lombard and Richmond Streets. They established the asylum to care for the orphans of the numerous immigrants who had died of cholera and typhus. It was open to children of all creeds and was situated in one of two houses that sat side by side and which were owned by Elmsley. Mrs. Patrick Lee, who also conducted a school for girls, was its first matron. In 1851, Mother Delphine Fontbonne and three other Sisters of St. Joseph took over the operation of the orphanage. They had traveled by stagecoach and boat from Philadelphia at the request of Toronto's Roman Catholic Bishop Armand de Charbonnel.

Girls' Home
The Girls' Home, built in 1868 at Gerrard Street East and Seaton Street. Today the only surviving section of the building is a union hall.

Money was scarce and the orphanage struggled for several years to survive, depending day to day on the charity of Torontonians of all religious denominations. By 1859, the Nelson Street orphanage became too small. The children were moved to the House of Providence, which had been built in 1857 on Power Street, next to the church "for the relief of the poor and destitute of all classes and creeds," according to its patron, Bishop de Charbonnel.

Most of the inhabitants of Cabbagetown were Irish Protestants. Because so many of those who received help and comfort at the House of Providence were of Orange stock, the place came to be known with affection and gratitude as the House of Protestants. In 1876, orphaned children were moved from the House of Providence to the newly opened Sacred Heart Orphanage at Sunnyside in the city's west end.

The Girls' Home

In 1856, Toronto's first public nursery opened its doors on Victoria Street. Over the next decade, the nursery, which eventually changed its name to The Girls' Home and Public Nursery, then simply The Girls' Home, moved to Albert Street and then to Carlton Street. In 1860, the organization would enlarge the scope of its care to include girls up to 14 years of age. It would obtain its charter in 1863 and operate independently for the next 63 years when, in 1926, it would merge with the Protestant Orphans' Home and Female Aid Society. In 1868, the Girls' Home moved to a newly constructed building situated on the south side of Gerrard Street East between Ontario and Seaton Streets on land donated by William Cawthra. In 1885, and then again some years later, donations by William Gooderham made it possible to add south and east wings to the building. And in 1909, a separate school building containing three classrooms, which were capable of accommodating eighty pupils, was erected.

The Boys' Home

The Boys' Home was set up in 1859 in response to the alarming increase in juvenile crime in the city. Boys between the ages of five and fourteen were taught a trade. The older ones were apprenticed to local merchants and craftsmen. Half of what they earned was paid to the Home and the remainder was banked for them.

Despite the efforts of the Protestant Orphans' Home, the Girls' and Boys' Homes, and the St. Joseph's Orphans' Home, to protect the city's children, large numbers of them continued to suffer execrable treatment at the hands of neglectful and abusive adults. In 1867, a Working Boys' Home was established followed a year later by a Newsboys' Home.

Infants' Home and Infirmary

Infanticide and baby farming – the boarding of dozens of infants in utterly squalid conditions – were facts of life in nineteenth century Toronto. And despite the efforts of numerous churches and benevolent societies to protect Toronto's children, much more needed to be done. Recognizing this, a group of philanthropic women and a number of the city's trained nurses were determined to do their part. They established the Infants' Home and Infirmary in a rented house on Caer-Howell Street. The nurses volunteered their off-duty time to the shelter where young mothers stayed for up to four months after delivering their babies. In an effort to reduce expenses and to increase the chances of survival for orphaned newborns in the Home, they encouraged the mothers to nurse one other child.

In 1876, the Infants' Home and Infirmary moved to 678 Yonge Street. It remained there until 1882, when a residence was built on St. Mary's Street on the site of a reservoir, which had to be drained so that construction could begin. When the water had been removed from the reservoir, the remains of several infants were discovered. Nothing could have underscored more poignantly the desperate need for child-protection agencies of this kind.

(1864-1935)

John Joseph Kelso's efforts ultimately led to the establishment of the Children's Aid Society.

A few years after the erection of the house on St. Mary's Street, John Joseph Kelso, a young police reporter working in Toronto, whose job took him to the worst of the city's slums, had become outraged at the plight of so many children forced into lives of panhandling and prostitution because of poverty. In 1887, Kelso founded the Toronto Humane Society for the prevention of cruelty to children and animals. The following year he inaugurated the Fresh Air Fund and the Santa Claus Fund, which sponsored trips for the children to Toronto Island and other amusement spots around the city and provided cheer for poor women. In 1891, Kelso became the province's first Superintendent of the Department of Neglected and Dependent Children, a position for which he was paid $500 less per year than he'd earned as a reporter. Such was the government's careless attitude to the needs of underprivileged children; they simply were not a public policy priority. That same year, he presided over the incorporation of the Children's Aid Society, an organization that would, in 1951, amalgamate with the Infants' Home and Infirmary.

In 1893, the provincial government of Ontario passed the Child Protection Act, which combined the Department of Neglected and Dependent Children with Children's Aid Societies, thereby providing for the protection, care and control of neglected and dependent children. The Act also included provisions for temporary shelters and foster care, which fore-shadowed, many years later, the end of apprenticeships and institutional care. Kelso would use this legislation, as a basis for much of his work in dealing with the problem of wholesale child immigration schemes that sprang up in the late nineteenth and early twentieth centuries, whereby children from British slums were imported into Canada and exploited as cheap labour.

In 1895, John Joseph Kelso organized Canada's first Conference on Child Saving. He later played a major role in the Protestant Orphans' Home, serving for 18 years on the Committee of Council between 1906 and 1924.

Family Day Care Services

The Salvation Army

The Salvation Army, which had come to Canada in 1882, began a long history of ministering to the underprivileged and unwanted of the city. In October 1888, the "Sally Ann" opened its first Rescue Home for Fallen Girls in Toronto under the direction of Mrs. Nellie Coombs. The organization would establish similar shelters in Montreal, Winnipeg and Victoria.

The Jewish Day Nursery and Orphanage

In the mid-nineteenth century, there were fewer than 20 Jewish families living in Toronto. Since they were a closely-knit group and were able to care for their own, they did not require an orphanage. But by the turn of the century, the number of Jewish immigrants in the city had grown significantly. Life was no less difficult for the Jewish poor than it was for any other cultural or ethnic group that composed the city's working class. There developed a need within Toronto's Jewish community for a day nursery and orphanage to care for children and to assist women during their pregnancies and after they had given birth. In 1909, the Jewish Day Nursery and Orphanage opened in a three-storey building on Elizabeth Street. It was also used as a dispensary and outpatient clinic for Jewish immigrants.

Regardless of their religious affiliations, all of Toronto's child care agencies had two things in common: lack of sufficient operating funds – a lack that was virtually ignored by the provincial government – and a desperate need for qualified personnel to adequately serve their constituencies. Pleas to Toronto City Council for money were often met with counter pleas that municipal dollars were too scarce. The belief persisted that charity was a private matter. Prior to the 1890s, no specialized department existed within the local government that was responsible for the distribution of welfare to the needy.

"Motherless"
Photographic copy is on display
in lobby of Family Day Care Services' head office.

150 Years of Caring for Children and Families

Discipline at the Home was as conservative
as the book of Rules and Regulations
that governed it.

Fortunately for the Protestant Orphans' Home and Female Aid Society, the mayor did have authority to grant money, and each year a substantial amount was made to the Home.

The Protestant Orphans' Home
– A Refuge for Friendless Children

According to the official rules of operation, the new Home would be a refuge for "friendless children of all denominations of the Protestant religion," though over the years, children of all religions would also be admitted.

Though it was a home for orphans, the term "orphan" included any child in need of care or protection. A mother may have died, leaving a working husband unable to care for their offspring; there may have been too many mouths to feed in one family and relief could only be had by placing one or more children in the Home. Perhaps both parents had to work in order to survive, and they'd pay the Home to care for their children. The names of many families appear on the records of a number of local agencies of the time. A significant percentage of the children who were admitted had at least one living parent to whom he or she might return once the Lady Managers had been assured that adequate care could once again be provided. Over the years, one in four of those children with at least one living parent would return home. A much smaller percentage would be adopted – in many cases years before formal adoption legislation existed, which is not to say that the Lady Managers approved such arrangements without careful thought and sufficient proof of the adoptive parents' good character and standing in the community. Most children, however, had neither a mother nor a father and were admitted to the Home on a first priority basis. Children with no father received second priority, and children with no mother, third.

The Home was established on the fundamental belief that children should not have to suffer deprivation, neglect, or exploitation in any form. The Lady Managers therefore set about to

Family Day Care Services

ensure that none of these evils would touch the children who came into their care, for once inside the orphanage fence they lived an almost cloistered existence – one that was overlaid with the strict religious convictions of the Church of England. Life on the street for some had been a no-holds-barred struggle for survival. Security, order, and moral rectitude had been absent from their young lives, but no longer. The rules by which the new institution would operate required that "discipline shall be strictly parental in its character, and the order of decorum of a well regulated family shall be carefully observed."

Girls and boys slept in separate dormitories and their waking hours were governed by adherence to a strict routine. During the summer months, the children were awakened at six in the morning and were put to bed by nine at night. In the winter, they rose at seven and retired no later than eight o'clock in the evening.

There was never any doubt in the minds of the Lady Managers that they were on a rescue mission, and they pursued it with a will. So concerned were they that the children might be easily drawn into lives of moral decadence – particularly those who had already been exposed to prostitution, drunkenness, and criminality – that they strictly controlled access to them. According to one directive, "No relative or friend shall interfere in the management of the children nor visit them except in the presence of the matron, nor at any time when such visits are disapproved of by the Lady Managers."

Nor were "gentlemen of the cloth" exempt from scrutiny, for the matron was instructed to be particularly vigilant when it came to members of the clergy and other strangers who might attempt to visit the Home without permission.

As a general rule, children were admitted to the Home only after the Lady Managers had received a formal application submitted through their secretary. The "election" of applicants was made at the Society's monthly meetings. However, the Lady Managers individually had the authority to admit a child on an interim basis until full approval was granted.

The corner stone of the Western Wing of the Orphan's Home and Female Aid Society was laid on Tuesday the 3 day of July A.D. 1860 By The Honorable and right Reverend John Strachan, Lord Bishop of Toronto

Children stayed at the Home until they were 12 years old, at which time girls became indentured domestic servants and boys were apprenticed to local tradesmen. Usually, the Lady Managers arranged these situations. However, friends of the children occasionally were granted the privilege of procuring positions for them as long as the Lady Managers approved. The children were indentured to Protestant families, or to widows or spinsters, but only to those of good character. Never was a child contracted to a tavern keeper or to the operator of a boarding house. And under no circumstances was a girl apprenticed to an unmarried man.

Those with whom the children were placed were required to feed and clothe them "in a fit and proper manner," commensurate with their station in life. It was not expected, therefore, that a boy indentured to a farmer should be dressed in the manner of a successful merchant's son, but it was expected that such a boy receive clean and serviceable, if secondhand, work clothing and one respectable suit that he might wear to church on Sunday. In addition to clothing and feeding the children, masters had to properly instruct them in a trade, ensure that they were taught how to read and write, and raise them in the Protestant religion.

Girls were indentured until they were 18, boys until they were 21. Their masters were required to report each year on the well-being of their apprentices, and to pay to the Society 15 shillings a year per child. The Society deposited the money in the bank and gave it to each child upon completion of his or her apprenticeship. If a master failed to make the annual remittance, the person who had recommended him to the Society (more often than not his own clergyman) would receive a stern request from the Lady Managers to encourage the defaulter to bring the account up to date. Few people dared to risk being embarrassed in such a manner.

Though life in the Home was regimented, it represented a welcome improvement over what most of the children had been used to. And while the three-storey brick building was plain to the point of austerity, it was still a refuge. Because money had been a major consideration, its designers favoured functionality over aesthetics. Thus there were few grace notes to be found anywhere. Nevertheless, the place was tidy, warm, and above all, safe. The children could look forward to being tucked into bed between clean sheets. And if the food was plainly prepared and presented, at least it was fresh and in sufficient supply. For afternoon tea, the children were given two slices of fresh bread, maple syrup, a tin cup of milk and fresh fruit in season.

The children received Protestant religious instruction, which included Sunday School taught by members of the Young Men's Christian Association. In addition, a schoolroom had been added to the orphanage and the city's school board provided a teacher.

Mrs. Holmes, the matron for the first 15 years that the orphanage was in operation, took direction from the Lady Managers who placed in her their utmost confidence. Accordingly, she was given full authority to run the orphanage as she saw fit. In matters of discipline, she was prosecutor, judge, jury and executioner. Her word was law. Correction, though strict, was tempered with affection and was never excessive. Each year at the Society's annual general meeting, the children – girls dressed in freshly pressed white pinafores and boys in dark tweed suits – offered up a hymn or two as part of the opening exercises.

Those with whom the children were placed
were required to feed and clothe them
"in a fit and proper manner," ….

Dollars and Cents

December 5, 1852, Ayr Advertiser

"The Lady Managers of the Protestant Orphans' Home acknowledge with many thanks, the following contributions kindly collected and forwarded by the Rev. Dr. Lett: – Daniel Manly, Esq., Ayr Mills, Ayr, a bag of flour; J. Goldie, Esq., Greenfield Mills, Ayr, a bag of flour; Mrs. Lett, Nightsleigh, Ayr, two pigs and two bags of potatoes; Mr. Backnell, Biefnheim, Ayr, a quarter of veal; Mr. White, Ayr, a quarter of mutton; Mr. Ross, Ayr, a large piece of beef."

December 12, 1862, The Globe

"Protestant Orphans' Home: – The Lady Managers of the Protestant Orphans' Home acknowledge with many thanks having received from Mr. Fisher, weighmaster, twelve rolls of butter taken for light weight, Dec. 6, and twenty loaves of bread also taken for light weight, Dec. 9; from Mr. Duncan Clarke five gallons of oil."

May 27, 1863, The Globe

"The Lady Managers of the Protestant Orphans' Home acknowledge with many thanks the following donations during the month: – From a friend, 12 boys' jackets, 12 vests, 11 pairs of trousers; Mrs. John Boulton, milk daily; Mrs. Crickmore, milk daily; Mr. Webb, a large loaf weekly; the butchers and market gardeners of St. Lawrence Market, meat and vegetables daily."

Well after the turn of the century, countless notices of this sort continued to appear in newspapers across Ontario. They testified to the basic goodness and generosity of country and city folk who sent what they could afford to help the Protestant Orphans' Home and Female Aid Society. While the largest gifts of land and money, which had come from the city's leading families, were most memorable and the subject of genuine gratitude, it was the daily,

Family Day Care Services

small donations of cash, food, farm produce, and clothing that permitted the matron and her staff to make ends meet. No gift was too small and nothing was wasted.

Occasionally, food arrived on the hoof, or still clucking. Fresh meat of any kind was a welcome addition to the menu. But because the matron and her staff seldom knew in advance when someone intended to make a gift of livestock to the Home, they had to be prepared to treat such donations as temporary guests of the Society until such time as the cook required their presence in the kitchen. Thereupon, they were unsentimentally dispatched, butchered, and transformed into nourishing meals.

December 27, 1863, the Daily Leader
"Protestant Orphans' Home – The treasurer of the Protestant Orphans' Home begs to acknowledge the following sums: – From District (Orange) Lodge (LOL), Derry West, per Mr. A. C. Irvine, $23.55; LOL No. 264, per Mr. W. Greenwood, $5; LOL No. 774, Brussels, Ontario, per Mr. James Young, treasurer, $5; collected by Mr. T. S. Jones, High Constable of York, from the Grand and Petit Jurors, Autumn Assizes, and Grand Jurors December Sessions, $22.50; LOL No. 1,184, Campbellville, per Mr. W. Caster Brooke $2.50."

The Odd Fellows, churches of all denominations, and the Orange Order regularly contributed money to the work of the Society. The Orangemen were especially faithful and generous in their contributions. On February 18, 1864, members of the Grand Lodge of the Loyal Orange Association and all the orphans in the Home attended a service at St. George's Church, which was led by Rev. Lett. After the service, at which a substantial amount of money was collected for the work of the Home, the Orangemen assembled outside the church and marched the short distance to the orphanage, where the new East, or Orange Wing was dedicated by Rev. Lett. Contributions made by Orangemen from all over Ontario had completely paid for the addition.

150 Years of Caring for Children and Families

From The Leader, June 9, 1864

> The annual meeting of the Protestant Orphans' Home was held last evening in the St. Lawrence Hall. There were present a large number of ladies and gentlemen immediately interested in the welfare of this admirable institution. The little orphans were seated on forms—the boys on one side of the platform and the girls on the other. They were well dressed and appeared remarkably clean and healthy.

From Globe and Mail, June 9, 1864

> The general annual meeting of the Protestant Orphans' Home and Female Aid Society was held last night in the St. Lawrence Hall. A few minutes before eight o'clock children in the number of 51 were marched into the hall. Their appearance reflected great credit upon the matron. The ...

The above are examples of early newspaper articles kept in Family Day Care Services' archives.

June, 1866, The Globe
"*Protestant Orphans' Home – The treasurer thankfully acknowledges a donation of ten dollars from Mr. G. N. Carlisle, proprietor of the "Terrapin Saloon," King Street, Toronto.*"

Philanthropists, churches and benevolent societies weren't the only ones who possessed a generous spirit.

June 8, 1866, The Globe
"*Protestant Orphans' Home – The Lady Managers thankfully acknowledge the following donations: – two bags of flour from the mayor of Toronto; vegetables from Mrs. Spratt; disinfectants from the health office; apples from Mrs. Foster; $2 from Mrs. G. L. Allen, for buying cakes; free admission of twenty children to the circus by Mr. Ritchie; apples and sweetmeats from Mr. Ritchie; free passage of children to the island by Capt. Salter; bread, butter and tea on the island by Mrs. Parkinson. The treasurer begs to acknowledge $2 collected by Mr. John McLean at a temperance meeting at Mount Pleasant.*"

June 3, 1874, The Leader
"*The Lady Managers also desire to return their thanks to the captain and owners of the City of Toronto (steamer) for a free trip given the children to Niagara; and to the captain of the steamer Bouquet for free trips to the island, which excursions were heartily enjoyed by the children.*"

August 23, 1877, The Globe
"*Protestant Orphans' Home – The entire number, at present 106, of the young pensioners of this charity had a grand picnic yesterday. The sport (sic) selected was High Park, and the party was conveyed thither in some dozen and a half cabs, the owners of which made the conveyance a free gift. The children were all neatly attired and presented a gratifying spectacle. They were accompanied by many of the active patrons of the Home, who directed and shared in the day's recreation. The day was spent in high enjoyment by the children, and will be a memorable event for them.*"

Toronto, 1877

Amelia was heartbroken as she watched the bigger children run ahead of her and scramble into the last cab in a line of 12 that waited on the street in front of the Sullivan Street Home. Each one was full of bouncing, squealing orphans who could barely contain their excitement at the thought of picnicking in High Park. But there seemed to be no room for Amelia. Hot tears stung her eyes and she bit her bottom lip to keep from crying. She was about to turn and run back into the orphanage, when a kindly voice said, "You can come up here and sit by me if you'd like, Missy. Help me drive old Chum." It was the cabman, smiling down at her.

Amelia looked wide-eyed at the driver, then up at the big white horse. She felt a hand on her shoulder and turned to find Miss Wheelright standing beside her. The kindly matron bent down and, scooping up the little girl, set her gently upon the black leather seat beside the driver. Proud as punch, Amelia smoothed her freshly laundered pinafore and beamed down at Miss Wheelright.

"You hold on tight up there, Amelia," said the matron.

"I ain't never drove a wagon before, Mister," said Amelia, breathless at the thought of handling the reins.

"That's alright, Missy," said the cabman, "I've never had a pretty girl sit up here beside me before."

Up ahead, the line of cabs began to move off down Sullivan Street toward Spadina Avenue, where they would turn north to Dundas Street, which would take them to the western suburbs of the city and High Park. When it was his turn, the cabman clucked his tongue. "Let's go, Chum," he said.

The big white horse lifted its head and leaned into the traces. With a slight lurch, the cab was off.

"There you go, Missy," said the cabman. "You can take over now." And he handed the little girl the reins, which hung slack across the horse's back. On the way, old Chum automatically turned when the other horses turned, and stopped when they stopped. In fact, he needed no direction.

Family Day Care Services

But Amelia was wonderfully innocent of that. As far as she knew, she had driven the cab and all the children in it to High Park. And she would remember the thrill that her special status had given her until she was a very old woman.

☙❧

The children looked forward to day trips to city parks and waterfront amusements. Ferry rides to the Toronto Islands were especially exciting. The archipelago of 15 tiny islands recently had been sculpted from a single peninsula that had jutted out into Lake Ontario by a violent storm that struck Toronto in 1858.

American showman and circus producer P.T. Barnum also earned the gratitude of the Lady Managers for giving the orphans free admission to his "grand exhibition of animals," which visited Toronto in 1874.

On occasion, drama societies and choral groups held fund raising events, the proceeds of which were given to local charities, including the Protestant Orphans' Home. Stage shows were a popular form of entertainment and a fairly reliable source of charitable funding. For example, on January 31, 1880, an amateur troupe of juveniles staged Gilbert and Sullivan's H.M.S. Pinafore at the St. Andrew's Church Hall (it had been staged professionally in London, England for the first time less than two years before). The Globe reported the following day, "The spacious room was crowded long before eight o'clock by the elite of the city, and by the time the curtain was rung up many were turned away, there not being standing room." Protestant Orphans' Home was among the charities to receive money from the proceeds of that production.

Family Day Care Services

December 15, 1886, The Mail
"The Lady Managers of the Protestant Orphans' Home commenced their 'All World's Fair,' in aid of the funds of the institution yesterday afternoon at three o'clock in the Adelaide Street rink, and it is almost safe to say that no previous event of the kind ever had so brilliant and successful an inauguration. The official opening was made by the Lieutenant-Governor...The rink presented a novel and charming appearance. Each side of the main floor was lined with a row of booths, most attractively decorated in striking contrasts of colour and representing various countries by which were collected either productions of these lands or articles suggestive of the inventive or industrial skill of their inhabitants. Each booth was in (sic) charge of a number of ladies attired in picturesque dresses of the characteristic type associated with the different countries, and in most cases it must be said that the imitation was very faithful except that in some instances, the material of the dresses was of a richer and costlier quality than is supposed to be worn by the classes represented. Silk, satin, and velvet were noticeable in the costumes of Spanish gypsy girls, French peasants, Turkish ladies, and Scotch lassies, but as these materials enhanced the rich effect of the arrangement of the colours the departure from strict accuracy was an improvement."

The Lady Managers were by no means shrinking violets when it came to raising money for the Home. They threw soirées and fancy dress balls at places such as the St. Lawrence Hall, the Horticultural Gardens Pavilion at Allan Gardens on Sherbourne Street, and the original King Street site of the city's new Crystal Palace, which was fashioned after the one built in London's Hyde Park. (Toronto's Crystal Palace would eventually be moved to the Exhibition grounds, just south of the Dufferin Gate.) These fundraising events were known for their artistry and flare. They never failed to attract not only the leading lights of the city, but representatives of senior levels of the government as well. The year following their successful "All World's Fair," with the help of the National Opera Company, the Lady Managers staged a production of "The White Slave," though in doing so, they attracted criticism from the city's Methodists. Unchastened by the scolding, the following year the Lady Managers threw a grand charity ball at the Horticultural Gardens Pavilion. Despite the fact that Governor-General and Lady Stanley and Mayor Clarke and Mrs. Clarke patronized the event, the Toronto clergy clucked their tongues in disapproval. Said Faith Fenton, writing in one of the Toronto papers, "Dancing is looked upon with such a severe eye by the clergy of Toronto that many prominent citizens are somewhat backward about giving their patronage to the few public balls that come off during the winter season. But when the subject of patronage is charity, Toronto has always been to the front, and the majority of our leading citizens are noted for their liberality when deserving objects are brought under their notice. Such an object was the charity ball in aid of the Protestant Orphans' Home... 'A charity ball.' The term is tossed somewhat disdainfully from the lips of the ultra-religionists, who, good people that they are, hear the footsteps of that 'roaring lion' (Satan) beneath the pulsing measure of the waltz, and see the gleam of his eyes 'seeking whom he may devour' beneath the glitter of the ballroom lights, nor think that this undesirable visitor may find a more congenial abode in the hearts filled with malice and uncharitableness."

Fenton did not confine her observations to the kerfuffle over dancing. She gave readers the benefit of her opinion concerning the style and quality of the costumes worn by the women who attended the ball, as well: *"The law of good taste was not violated in any one instance that I could see – and I wore my spectacles!"*

Over the years, there would be many operettas, concerts, bazaars and fancy balls in aid of the Home. They were popular events on the social calendar of the city's elite.

Some of the 400 guests at the fancy-dress ball in aid of the Protestant Orphans' Home, held in April, 1870, in the Toronto Music Hall, at the corner of Church and Adelaide Streets—the building that was later to become the Public Library. The gentleman in Highland dress, in left foreground, is Capt. Prince; 2, Miss Amy Grant; 3, Major Burstall; 4, Miss Gussie Ridout; 11 and 12, Mrs. Beckett and Mrs. Banks, the beautiful McPherson sisters; bowing to them, Mr. Jacobi; 16, Mr. James Michie, in Highland dress; 22, Mrs. W. P. Howland; 24, Miss Essie Heward (later Mrs. Stikeman); to her left, the young hopeful in knee breeches is Stephen Jarvis, Jr.; beside him, Mr. Frank Heward. Others in this interesting group include Sir Casimir Gzowski, Sir D. L. McPherson, Mrs. Northey, Mr. Sam Nordheimer, Mr. Chris Baines, Mr. Nicol Kingsmill, Mr. and Mrs. Henry Cawthra, Mr. Walter Cassells, Mr. and Mrs. J. S. McMurray

Family Day Care Services

Suffer the Little Children

From 1854 until well into the 1880s, Doctor William Winslow Ogden was the chief attending physician to the Protestant Orphans' Home. For more than 30 years, he was known for the diligence and cheerfulness with which he performed his duties at the Home. And though every year at the Society's annual general meeting the Board recognized the debt they owed him, he refused to charge a fee.

Dr. Ogden was a young man when he first offered his services to the Home. In time, he became a highly respected senior member of the city's medical community, teaching medical jurisprudence at the Toronto School of Medicine. When the medical faculty of the University of Toronto was established, he was appointed professor of forensic medicine. Despite the many demands placed on his time, his devotion to the Sullivan Street orphans never waned.

By the mid 1880s, Doctors MacDonald, McConnell and Spragge joined Ogden in managing the increased medical workload at the Home, the result of larger enrollments. All of them were leaders in their profession and ran busy practices, yet they regarded as a priority the care they freely gave to the Society's children. The same could be said for Dr. James Ross, the attending physician of the Girls' Home for more than 20 years. Ross was an accomplished surgeon and a specialist in midwifery who, in 1889, was elected president of the Canadian Medical Association. Near the turn of the century, other names were added to the list of those physicians who came to the aid of the Home – among them Doctors Brown, Hodder, Grace, Sheard, Albert, Hunter, Sterling, Ryerson, Bowles, McKinley, Price Brown and Livingston. Until the mid-to-late 1920s, when the Society made the transition from institutional to foster care, the doctors played an essential role in the health and overall well-being of the orphan children.

The mortality rate among small children, especially those who lived in crowded slums, was high in nineteenth-century Toronto.

Common childhood illnesses such as measles and whooping cough frequently proved fatal. However, once a child was brought into the Home where he or she received properly prepared meals on a regular basis, slept in a clean bed, and was expected to maintain a much higher level of personal hygiene than perhaps might have been previously practiced, the risk of death from such diseases fell dramatically. For the most part, residents of the Home who became ill made full recoveries. Only rarely did any of them succumb to their illness. In January 1866, however, 46 children were confined to bed when measles and whooping cough swept through the Home.

At a meeting of the Society held on Tuesday, January 30, 1866, the secretary recorded events as follows:

"The secretary regrets to state that since the last meeting, there has been, and still is, much sicknefs (sic) in the Home, children having been received into the Home who brought with them whooping cough, which spread among the children, and before they recovered from that disease, were attacked with measles, and now I am grieved to say are suffering most fearfully from dysentery. The mortality has been very great, 16 of our poor little orphans have died during this month. Dr. Ogden has been most attentive, giving his time and advice, and doing all in his power to stop the disease and alleviate their suffering.

By early February, 18 children had died.

Sarah Harris............nine years......died January 6/66.......measles & whooping cough

Thomas Innocent.......four years......died January 7/66.......measles & whooping cough

John Henry Peters......five years.......died January 13/66.....measles & dysentery

Matilda Talbot..........four years......died January 13/66.....measles & whooping cough

Thomas McDonald.....five years.......died January 15/66.....measles & whooping cough

Samuel Cunningham...three years.....died January 16/66.....measles & dysentery

Sarah McClellan........four years......died January 19/66.....measles & whooping cough

Richard Harris..........eleven years....died January 20/66.....measles & whooping cough

William McClellan......ten years.......died January 21/66.....measles & dysentery

John Chase..............four years......died January 22/66.....whooping cough & dysentery

George Innocent........six years........died January 23/66.....measles & dysentery

Robert Winters..........six years........died January 23/66.....measles & dysentery

John Irwin...............five years.......died January 25/66.....measles & dysentery

William Glavin..........three years.....died January 25/66.....measles & dysentery

Soloman Pennant.......six years........died January 27/66.....measles & dysentery

Joshua Fox..............six years........died January 29/66.....measles & dysentery

David Wiggin...........four years......died January 31/66.....measles & dysentery

Lavinia McClellan......eight years.....died February 3/66.....measles & dysentery

Names of the 18 children who died from illnesses in 1866.

Because of his large workload, Dr. Ogden had called in other physicians to help him manage the crisis. They found that poor drainage at the Home had confounded their efforts to nurse the children back to health. To prevent further outbreaks, the physicians agreed that all the children would have to be temporarily housed elsewhere, and that the entire building would have to be thoroughly ventilated, cleansed, and drained. The domestic staff took every measure they could to sanitize the building.

Those children who recovered and those who had not taken ill were moved out of the Sullivan Street Home. Along with furniture and utensils from the Home, the children were loaded onto drays provided at no charge by the Grand Trunk and the Great Western Railway companies and driven to another home in the city where they would stay for two months while the orphanage was put right. The sudden and tragic loss of eighteen children between the ages of three and eleven dealt a terrible blow to everyone involved. Doctor Ogden, the matron, Mrs. Holmes, and her small staff, and many of the Lady Managers worked themselves almost to the point of exhaustion trying to save those who were dying, and to preserve the health and safety of the remaining children. The incident stands as one of the saddest in the entire history of the Society, which deserved its enviable reputation as a well-run institution.

Dr. Ogden had sought to avoid precisely such an occurrence when, the previous year, he had recommended that two bedrooms on the second floor of the Home be made into an infirmary. It would be segregated from the rest of the building and have its own staircase leading from the ground floor. The Board had seen the wisdom in his recommendation and, at the cost of $114, had finished the renovations. The outbreak of 1866, however, caught everyone off guard. The new infirmary was simply inadequate, and the infection had spread throughout the building before anything could be done to prevent it.

Mrs. Holmes was so distraught at the loss of the children that she tearfully offered to leave the Home. But the Lady Managers knew the devoted matron was not to blame and refused to accept her resignation. Ultimately, however, the tragedy took its toll on Mrs. Holmes and she retired from the Home.

One newspaper, the Toronto Watchman, launched a vicious attack on the Society, alleging that the Home was mismanaged, that its directors had deliberately attempted to disguise the organization's Protestant affiliation, and that the matron who had been hired to replace Mrs. Holmes, a Mrs. Kelly, was married to a Roman Catholic. (The allegations were proven groundless, but the notion of the spouse of a Roman Catholic being employed by the Home clearly offended the editor of the Toronto Watchman.) The stern response of a special committee set up to answer the newspaper's accusations are recorded in the minutes of the monthly meeting, held Tuesday, February 27, 1866:

"*Your committee have not had before them sufficient evidence to report definitely and decisively upon the other charges as to the maladministration of the internal economy of the Home, but such testimony as they have had is thoroughly satisfactory leading them to the belief that these charges are equally false as the two previous ones. In fact, they are too absurd and ridiculous to be true.*

"*Your committee have no hesitation in recording their opinion that the charge against the managers is a grofs (sic) libel on these excellent ladies. Your committee have reason to believe that the retiring matron, Mrs. Holmes, has sustained to the last the high character which has been accorded to her in various of the annual printed reports of the Society.*

"*Your committee have had before them the statement of Dr. Ogden Esq., M.D., the medical officer of the Home, and by it they are confirmed in their belief that there has been no carelefsnefs (sic) or culpable inattention on the part of the officials of the Home, except for one of the nurses, who has been discharged.* (Neither the nurse's identity nor the reason for her dismissal are mentioned in the minutes.)

"*It seems to your committee that some member of the institution, a dismissed servant perhaps, carries false and malicious complaints to the editor of the Watchman, who they regret to say affords too ready a vehicle*

1925

PROTESTANT ORPHAN HOME

TO THE EDITOR OF THE LEADER.

Sir,—I ask the privilege of calling the attention of the numerous readers of your influential journal to the present condition and claims of the above named institution. It was the …

Ever since the epidemic, which carried off eighteen of the children in 1866 they have been cramped for means to carry on the institution ; and now, that they have lately had sixteen of the children sick with typhoid fever, their funds are exhausted, and they have had to borrow money to meet their daily expenditure. Unwilling to shut the door on any destituted Protestant orphan, born in wedlock, the ladies have had under their care at one time lately no less than one hundred and two orphan children, and eve now the children in the institution number no less than sixty-six.

The ladies deem it only necessary to have these …

Grave Marker
"Suffer the little children to come unto me."

for their publicity by giving them insertions in his paper.

"Signed William Adamson, John McKee, J.R. Brownlee, James B. Lindsay, and D'Arcy Boulton."

It is not known for certain where the 18 children were buried, though it is likely that they would have been interred in paupers' graves. In 1876, the Society purchased six lots in the northwest corner of St. James Cemetery, at Parliament and Bloor Streets, so that the children of families who had no plot could be properly buried. A sandstone monument was erected and on the front was engraved: *"This monument was erected by some of the children of the Orphans' Home to the memory of their little companion Rebecca Dorrington who died June 7, 1868 Aged 6 years – Suffer little children to come unto me."*

By the time the Protestant Orphans' Home sold the lots to the Children's Aid Society in 1962, the names of 28 children had been engraved on the monument.

The Need to Expand

By 1882, it had become clear that the Sullivan Street Home could no longer accommodate the growing number of children resident there. Moreover, the Society had received a substantial increase in the number of applicants for admission. A search was made of the city for a suitable lot on which to build a new and much larger orphanage that could house 125 children. One costing $7,500 was found on the west side of Dovercourt Road, two blocks south of College Street.

The laying of the corner stone for the new orphanage took place on Saturday, October 7, 1882. Rev. Thomas Fuller, Lord Bishop of Niagara, presided over the ceremony, which represented a major event in the city. The new Home was decidedly grander and more expensive than the one on Sullivan Street. In fact, it would cost the Society between forty and forty-five thousand dollars. A full description of the proposed structure that appeared in one of the local newspapers ran, in part, as follows:

Family Day Care Services

"The new building, which will be of red brick, will have a solid stone foundation. The centre portion will be three storeys high and the wings two storeys. This exclusive of the basement, which is only four feet below the ground line and constitutes another storey.... The style will be modern English, giving a pleasing effect without any unnecessary expenditure for ornamentation, the principal object aimed at being compactness, convenience of arrangement, and solidity of structure."

The newspaper article went on to describe in detail the dormitories, hallways, and various special purpose rooms that had been incorporated into the design. The Lady Managers who attended the corner stone ceremony were understandably proud of their new orphanage – so was Mayor McMurrich, who addressed the crowd on behalf of the Ladies and provided a verbal history of the Protestant Orphans' Home.

One year and one week later, on October 15, 1883, the children were led through the front door of their new residence at 344 Dovercourt Road. At the official opening ceremonies in November, special mention was made of the ongoing and generous contribution made to the Home since its inception by members of the Orange Order.

Over the entrance to the bright and airy dormitories of the Dovercourt orphanage was the commemorative inscription, "Blessed is he that considereth the poor and needy," which honoured the generosity of William Gooderham, who donated much of the furnishings of the sleeping quarters. Colourful lettering that had been carefully rendered by the boys of the Home encircled the head of each of the small white beds.

Gooderham, who was known for his philanthropy, was a friend to both the Girls' Home and the Protestant Orphans' Home. At one annual meeting of the Society, he publicly chided certain members of the local clergy for failing to demonstrate support and leadership by not attending the meeting. He also lambasted those upper class Torontonians who failed to donate money to the Home, calling them "dishonest." But he praised the generosity of the city's

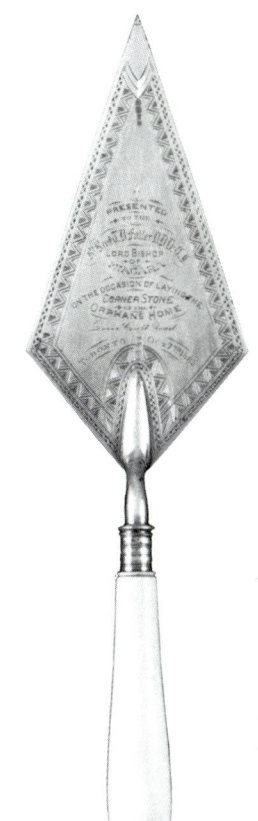

THE CEREMONY.

A silver trowel was then handed to the Bishop of Niagara, who duly performed the ceremony of laying the stone and dedicating the building to the purposes of the charity. Glass jars containing a twenty-five, a ten, and a five-cent piece of the coinage of 1882, copies of THE MAIL, *Globe*, and other newspapers, the *Dominion Churchman*, and *Orange Sentinel*, Orphans' Home reports, and list of officers were placed within the stone. Near it was displayed the flag of Norway and Sweden, out of compliment to the singer whose generous gift gave such an impetus to the Home.

150 Years of Caring for Children and Families

53

Dovercourt Orphans' Home
The Dovercourt orphanage, which was built in 1882, could accommodate 125 children.

"comparatively poor people" from whom the bulk of the money to run the institution came.

The children themselves contributed to the daily operation of the orphanage by performing domestic chores. The older boys helped out in the laundry while the girls knitted and sewed. The Home had its own sewing room and the matron was grateful for the donation of cast-off clothing. The girls were taught to transform old clothes and scraps of material into skirts, dresses for themselves and suits and everyday trousers for the boys. Each child received two good outfits a year. Used boots and shoes, donated to the institution, were also welcome.

The building featured well-equipped boys' and girls' gymnasiums, and a nursery, which accepted toddlers under three years of age. The little ones were not permitted to mingle with the older children.

An 1897 newspaper column entitled "Woman's Kingdom – Kit's Gossip" drew a picture of life at the Dovercourt Home:

"I was glad for the Orphans' Home when I saw Miss Deacon (the matron). We went from one room to another. We saw the refectory, or dining room, where two small mothers – I mean chicks, of course, but I cannot find words in which to picture the maternal attitude of them – were filling the mugs with water scooped from a bucket. We saw the kitchen, with great joints of beef simmering in deep pans of gravy; we saw the baker's shop piled with loaves; the larder stuffed with good things – not one thing superfluous – but all things needful. We saw the long, large, sunny dormitories, with their neat little iron bedsteads covered with white quilts and fitted with everything clean, sweet, and fitting. We looked into great presses and found stacks of stockings done up in shop parcels; bales of cloth for winter wear; rolls of calico and muslin for underwear and 'pinnies' and indeed aplenty of everything. Three sewing women were at work upon small breeches and skirts. There is no lack of material; no stint of anything, and yet this institution is run – I am told – and fully believe, on the most economic principles, costing a third less than anything of the kind in Toronto. Good management you see."

William Gooderham Sr.
(1790–1881)

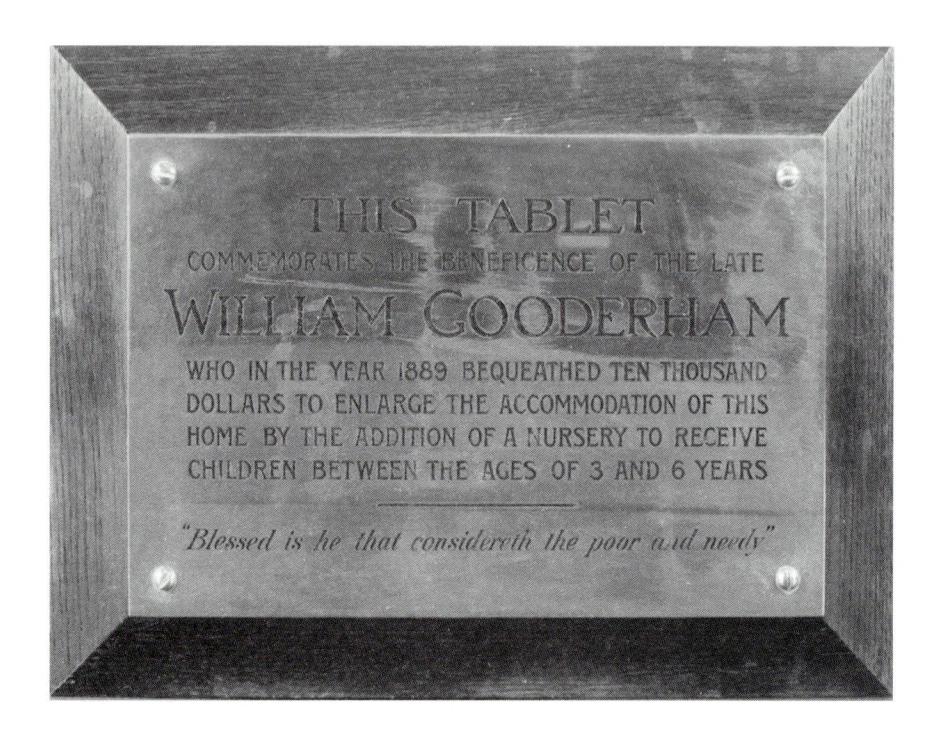

Gooderham & Worts Ltd.

Distiller and philanthropist, William Gooderham believed the Toronto clergy and members of the city's upper crust ought to have done far more than they had to help destitute children and their families.

GOODERHAM & WORTS, LTD.
TORONTO, CANADA.
CANADIAN RYE WHISKY

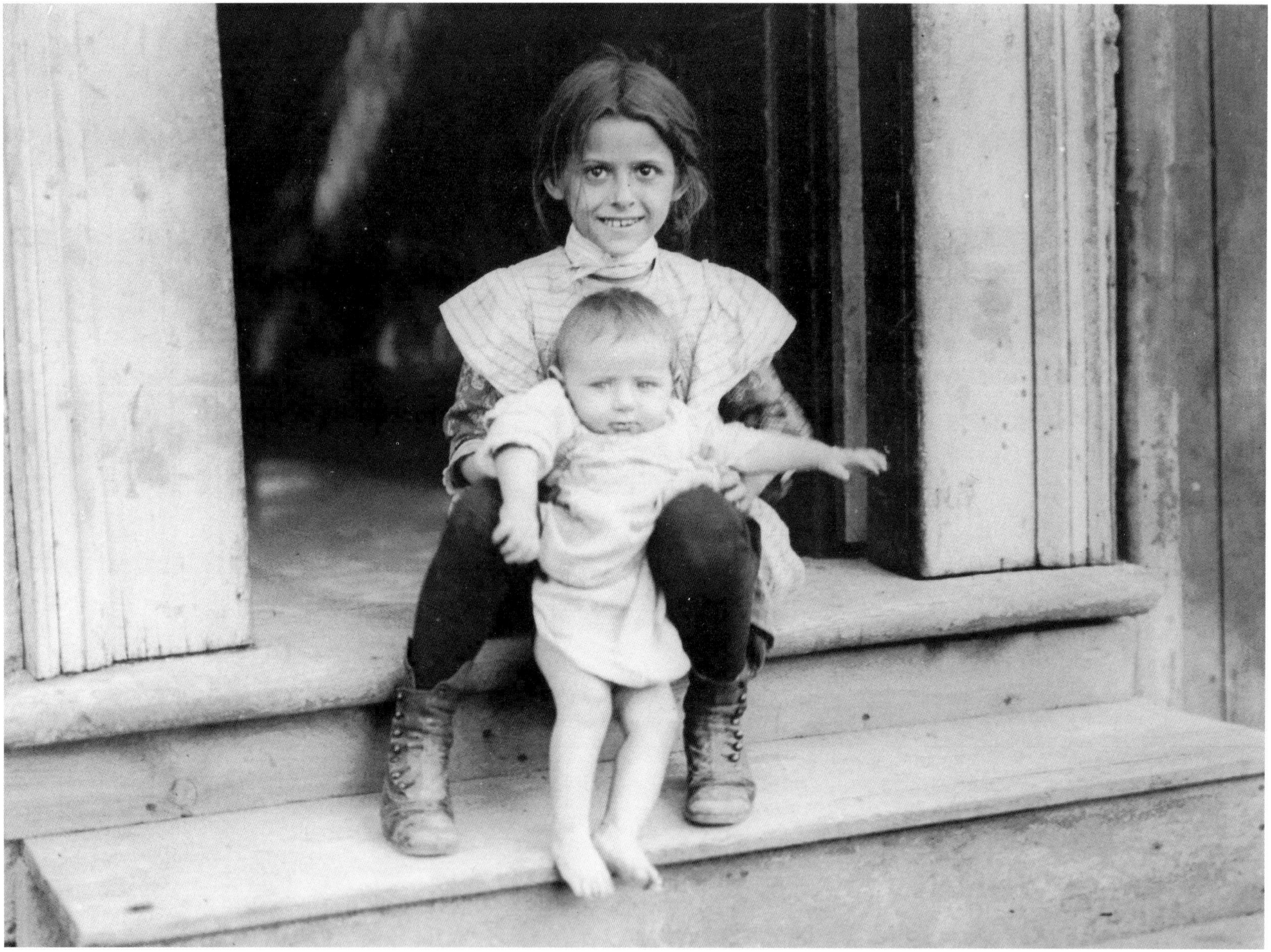

73 Yorkville Avenue
June 10th, 1899

I am writing a few lines hoping that all are well. And getting along very nicely. I like my place very well. I hardly ever get scolded. And I go lots of places. They are very kind to me. And I have not broke a dish since I've been here. And I go to Sunday School. The picnic is the 15 of June. And we are going to Long Branch. The Street is very quiet. And hardly any noise. And on the 2nd of June I went to the Queens park. All of the Girls in day School gave one cent in. And one of the teachers bought a basket of roses. And put them in the Queens park. Next door to us there is a piano. And the lady plays some very nice pieces. And I don't half to much work. But I don't mind it. I have a little room all to my self. And a little bed. I have all of my cards up on the wall. And they look very nice. And I know quite a few Girls at School. Some times a little Girl comes in are yard and plays with me. We tell each other all about the flowers. And I often go over to Yonge Street on a message. I think that's all this time.

Good bye
Send my love to all
Mrs Canfield
Miss McMillian
Miss McKee
And Miss McMaster a
and lots to your
Self
Your loving
Friend Rosie

"Blessed is he that considereth the poor and needy."

The Dovercourt Road Home would remain in operation for 43 years. In 1926, the Toronto Board of Education would purchase it for $50,000 and turn it into an all-girls institution called the Edith L. Groves School. The building was finally torn down in 1961, and in its place the Board of Education erected the all-girls Heydon Park Secondary School.

Up until the final years of World War I, Toronto's child care agencies had worked independently of one another. Cooperation between them had been negligible. Furthermore, municipal authorities had never imposed upon them rules to regulate their spending or means of operation. They had been left very much on their own. In 1917, however, Protestant Orphan's Homes joined numerous other social agencies in the Federation for Community Services. Joint fund raising and budgeting under the Federation umbrella offset, to some degree, the agency's loss of autonomy.

In 1921, the Child Welfare League of America conducted a survey of Toronto's child protection agencies and concluded that there was a need for some form of consolidation. Three years later, Protestant Orphan's Homes, The Girls' Home and The Boys' Home conducted a joint survey of their own. The resulting report challenged the boards of the three agencies to implement modern social work methods, to reorganize themselves and to forsake traditional, outworn policies and procedures. Moreover, the authors of the report recommended that the three agencies amalgamate if they hoped to continue to properly serve the needs of Toronto's dependent and neglected Protestant children. The needs of Jewish and Roman Catholic children were met by their own agencies. The survey concluded that the proposed organization should specialize in short term boarding care of children who were not wards of the city, and of convalescent and problem children who could not receive proper care in their own homes. Every effort, the report stated, would be made to keep the children with relatives. An amalgamated agency would abandon forever "congregate care" in favour of smaller institutional facilities that would supplement and

This plaque, which is on display in Family Day Care Services' head office, reminds of all the people who gave for the sake of the children.

provide quarantine and reception facilities for a network of 12 to 15 boarding homes – rented houses in suitable sections of the city. These would be centrally supervised and controlled, and would hold no more than 12 children. Each would have its own house mother and cook. There would be a reception home that would serve both as an administrative headquarters and a quarantine residence for newly received children who, for sound reasons, should not be immediately assigned to a boarding home.

The report suggested that the board of the newly constituted organization would be composed of representatives of all three agencies and number no more than 12 people. An executive director would be responsible for both administration and social work, and would be assisted by two supervisors, one for homes and the other for home-finding and child-placing.

The authors of the report recognized that the proposed undertaking would be unprecedented in Toronto, both in terms of service delivery methods and budget. But it did promise to serve the needs of the city's dependent and neglected children better than current methods of congregate care had done. And as for financial considerations, the operating budget of the proposed amalgamated agency would be no more than the combined budgets of all three agencies.

At the time of the group report's release, rapid urbanization had resulted in higher rates of employment among the working class. Their improved prospects meant fewer poor people. And while those who remained were as destitute as ever, a higher percentage of Toronto's poor tended to keep their children at home. Significant improvements in the supply of safe water, public health, hygiene, and disease control contributed to a decline in the number of people who became seriously ill and died. The number of children requiring the care of child rescue agencies began to decrease. In addition, the inauguration of mother's allowance and the opening of a home to care for soldiers' children, during and after the war years, meant that both Protestant Orphans' Home and the Girls

Home – indeed, all of the child care agencies – received fewer applications for admission. The number of children housed in these institutions steadily began to decline. Though the Girls' Home could accommodate up to 100 children, by 1925, only 63 girls lived there. There were even fewer children living in the Protestant Orphans' Home, which had been built to house 200. Despite reduced enrollment, the costs of operating both Homes continued to rise.

Some of the members of the Board of the Protestant Orphans' Home also sat on the Girls' Home Board, which simplified merger discussions. At the annual general meeting of the Girls' Home, which took place on November 6, 1925, an announcement was made that, under an act of the provincial government in May of the next year, the two organizations would become one and be known as Protestant Children's Homes. Merger with the Boys' Home, which had also been seriously considered, did not take place because the Board of that organization decided to continue on its own.

No longer needed, the Dovercourt Road orphanage was sold in 1926 to the Toronto Board of Education and the girls were moved to the former Girls' Home at 229 Gerrard Street East. The boys from Dovercourt took up residence at numbers 12 and 14 Pembroke Street. Money from the sale of the Home was invested in mortgages and provided the Agency with a substantial income.

For several years, the realization had been a growing among those involved in child rescue work, and to some extent among members of the public, that no matter how well an institution might be run, it could never replace the individual attention a child could receive in a private home. This belief, which had been underscored in the 1924 joint survey report, together with reduced institutional enrollment and rising costs, precipitated a major shift in the way the agency would serve children.

Moreover, from a health standpoint, the boarding of children in separate family homes instead of in a single large institution made

Black metal box for storing a girl's personal belongings at the Girls' Home, circa 1900.

November 7, 1925

FEWER APPLICATIONS AT ORPHANS' HOMES

Decision to Amalgamate Announced at Girls' Home Meeting.

CHANGED CONDITIONS

Child Welfare Work in Toronto Has Entered on New Phases.

Announcement was made yesterterday afternoon at the 69th annual meeting of the Girls' Home, 229 Gerrard Street east, of the decision to amalgamate the two corporations of the Protestant Orphans' Home and the Girls' Home. The latter is to be retained as it is for the residence of the girls of both institutions. It will also be used for administration purposes by the new corporation.

The growth of the city and the many changes made in carrying on child-welfare work, including the inauguration of mothers' allowances and the opening of homes for soldiers' children, had contributed to the shortage of applications for admission to the Girls Home, the Boys' Home and the Protestant Orphans' Home. The cost of maintenance of these large buildings had increased. By amalgamation, it was believed

---

good sense. At one meeting, the Agency's Director of Social Work, Kathleen Gorrie, told Board Members that the 41 children who still occupied the Gerrard Street Home had, in a single year, spent a cumulative total of 517 days in the Toronto Isolation Hospital, while during the same period, the 132 children who had been placed in foster homes spent only 164 days in the hospital – twelve days of hospitalization per home child versus less than two days per foster child.

From 1925 to 1930, foster care, or "boarding out," gradually replaced institutional care. But finding and supervising foster parents who were willing to provide much needed emotional support in clean, wholesome surroundings where the children might flourish took special skills – the sorts of skills that professional social workers possessed.

In the spring of 1929, only 40 children remained in institutional care in the Home at 229 Gerrard Street East. Another 130 had been placed in carefully selected foster homes in Toronto and in nearby rural areas. They were visited on a regular basis by Protestant Children's Homes workers, who paid particular interest to their health, schooling, and social development.

In November of 1929, Miss Gorrie, who had recently returned from a tour of child protection agencies in Baltimore, Boston, New York, and Philadelphia, reported that American agencies had forsaken institutional child care, and had instead embraced foster care as an eminently preferable mode of delivering their service. With the number of children in institutional care rapidly declining and operating costs escalating, did it make sense, she asked the Executive Committee, to keep the Gerrard Street Home open? When asked by a director how long it would take to find foster homes for the remaining 22 children in the Home, Miss Gorrie replied that she and her staff had already selected several suitable prospective homes and had made plans for the children to be placed in them by January of the following year. At a meeting held on November 19, 1929, the Board voted unanimously to close the

Gerrard Street Home. By January 14, 1930, all of the children in the care of the Agency had been placed in foster homes, marking the end of an era that had lasted 79 years.

At the same board meeting, after outlining the considerable amount of work performed by her small staff, Miss Gorrie pressed her case for three more social workers and an automobile that, she said, would make finding and supervising foster homes far less expensive. "The investigations of children and foster home applicants, home findings, and supervision have increased tremendously and case workload is steadily growing," she said. Workers were now counselling the parents of the children who came into care in an effort to keep families together. The Board became convinced that additional trained staff was required. Miss Gorrie's requests were soon honoured.

The change in the mode of service delivery necessitated a change in the public's perception of Protestant Children's Homes, from that of an orphanage to a modern, professionally run child care agency. And that shift in image proved to be difficult, as indicated by the headline of a 1929 article that appeared in the *Mail and Empire*, which read, "Difficult to Annihilate the Old Idea of Home-Child in Gingham 'Pinny.'"

"The old conception of the 'home child' in the gingham pinny has not entirely disappeared," Miss Gorrie told the reporter. "But our best weapon against it is to provide to the children simple, attractive, up-to-date clothing."

Parents who had hitherto been reluctant to place their children in an institution welcomed the notion of temporarily placing them in a well run and supervised boarding or foster home. Three-fifths of the children admitted to care in 1929 had not come from broken homes, but from unsatisfactory arrangements made by parents seeking to avoid institutional placement. In increasing number, such parents began to place their confidence in Protestant Children's Home to get them through difficult periods in the lives of their families.

Because there was no longer a need for the Gerrard Street East Home, it was leased to the Ascension Brotherhood Crusaders (soon to be known as the Toronto Men's Hostel), which used it to house indigent men during the Great Depression. In 1940, the Board put the Gerrard Street Home on the market, but it wasn't until the summer of 1947 that the Toronto Men's Hostel finally purchased it. The school wing became a community hall and would, many years later, become a union hall. Eventually the main building was levelled and the land turned into a Brewer's Retail parking lot.

When an agreement with the Ascension Brothers was reached, the agency purchased a house located at 28 Selby Street, which was outfitted with offices, reception rooms, and a clinic. It would serve as the agency's headquarters until 1947, when the agency moved to new quarters at 380 Sherbourne Street, across from Allan Gardens.

Selby Street Office
The Agency occupied 28 Selby Street from 1930 to 1947.

The Orphans' Home

Patrons & Patronesses
Her Excellency the Countess of Elgin and Kincardine,
    1851 – 1855
Her Excellency Lady Head, 1856 – 1861
Her Excellency Lady Monck, 1862 – 1868
Her Excellency Lady Young, 1869 – 1872
Her Excellency The Countess of Dufferin, 1873 – 1878
His Excellency The Marquess of Lorne
    (Governor General of Canada), 1879 – 1883
Her Royal Highness Princess Louise, 1879 – 1883
His Excellency Lord Lansdowne
    (Governor General of Canada), 1884 – 1888
The Marchioness of Lansdowne, 1884 – 1888
Lord Stanley of Preston (Governor General of Canada),
    1889 – 1892
Lady Stanley of Preston, 1889 – 1892
The Earl of Derby, 1893
The Countess of Derby, 1893
The Earl of Aberdeen (Governor General of Canada),
    1894 – 1900
The Countess of Aberdeen, 1894 – 1900
The Earl of Minto (Governor General of Canada),
    1901 – 1904
The Countess of Minto, 1901 – 1904

Patrons & Patronesses
The Earl Grey (Governor General of Canada), 1905 – 1911
The Countess Grey, 1905 – 1911
H.R.H The Duke of Connaught
    (Governor General of Canada), 1912 – 1916
H.R.H. The Duchess of Connaught, 1912 – 1916
His Excellency The Duke of Devonshire
    (Governor General of Canada), 1917 – 1921
Her Excellency The Duchess of Devonshire, 1917 – 1921
General, The Lord Byng
    (Governor General of Canada), 1922 – 1926
Her Excellency Lady Byng, 1922 – 1926

Honourary Patronesses
Mrs. Ludlow, 1870 – 1872
Mrs. Howland, 1870 – 1886
Lady MacPherson, 1870 – 1893
Mrs. Murray, 1881 – 1885
Mrs. A. Cameron, 1889 – 1895
Mrs. Morrow, 1895 – 1914

Honourary Presidents
Mrs. Vancoughnet, 1897 – 1899
Mrs. John Cawthra, 1895, 1901 – 1912

150 Years of Caring for Children and Families

Protestant Children's Homes

1926–1971

Protestant Children's Homes Prayer

O God, from whom all holy desires,
all good counsels and all just works
do proceed, we beseech Thee to direct
our consultations and to prosper with
Thy blessing the designs of this Society.

Grant wisdom and faithfulness to its
directors and comfort with Thy grace those
benefactors who contribute to its support.

Bless the children who are under its
foster care and may thy Holy Spirit
guide all who are responsible for the
well-being of their souls and bodies,
through Jesus Christ, our Lord.

Amen

Gull Lake, Muskoka 1928

Judith stood shivering with her toes gripping the edge of the dock. She trembled more from excitement than from cold, for this morning she was determined to plunge in and paddle for everything she was worth to where Miss Carr stood, 10 feet away, chest-deep in the chilly, amber water of the lake.

Each morning for the past week, Miss Carr had stood patiently in the same spot – sometimes for as long as 20 minutes – arms outstretched and smiling through blue lips and chattering teeth as she coaxed the little girl to swim to her. And each morning, Judith had remained rooted to the dock, unable to force herself to jump in.

"Come on, Judith, you can do it! I'll catch you. Don't worry," Miss Carr would call.

All her life, thought Judith, grownups had made promises to her that they hadn't kept. Why should Miss Carr be any different?

Each day, the little girl's courage had failed her. Her face would contort in a spasm of anguish as tears of frustration flowed down her cheeks. Defeated, she would run in shame from the dock and along the footpath in search of a quiet corner in which to hide. Inevitably, Miss Carr would find her and encourage her to try again the following morning.

"I'll be there, Judith. I won't let you sink."

"This morning, I'm going to do it!" Judith told herself. She struggled to stop shaking, but it was no use; her knees would not stop knocking together.

"I'm here, Judith. You go ahead and jump and I'll catch you."

"You'll catch me? You promise?"

"I promise!"

This time, there'd be no tears, no shame, no running away. Judith took a huge gulp of breath, pinched her nose with one hand and, holding the other hand aloft, launched herself into the air, where it seemed to her that she hung suspended for an eternity before plunging seat-first into the

150 Years of Caring for Children and Families

71

cold water. A second or two later, she bobbed up, a tangle of flailing arms and churning legs. Nearby, she heard Miss Carr calling, "Kick, Judith! Kick!"

The little girl kicked her legs and pulled frantically at the water with her arms until, to her surprise, she found that she was keeping her head above the surface.

"Kick! That's the girl, kick!"

Then a strong hand caught Judith's and pulled her through the water. The little girl flung her arms around Miss Carr's neck and held her fast. "She told me she'd catch me, and she did," thought Judith.

Each day thereafter, Miss Carr stood a little farther from the dock. And each day, Judith plucked up her courage and forced herself to trust — not only Miss Carr, but herself. By the time Judith returned to the city, she had learned much more than how to swim.

In March 1927, the Chairman of Protestant Children's Homes received a letter from a summer resident of the Muskoka Lakes district named Mrs. Alderson, offering to sell 36 acres of land situated on the east shore of Gull Lake, near Gravenhurst. Her asking price was $3,500. For a number of years, the Agency had paid the Children's Aid for the privilege of sending girls and boys to that organization's summer camp at Bronte. But the offer of land in Muskoka provided the Agency with an opportunity to establish its own summer camp. In April, as soon as the spring melt cleared the roads of snow and the lakes of ice a small delegation headed north to inspect the property and the buildings on it. Upon their return, they recommended that the Board purchase the property at Mrs. Alderson's asking price so that Camp Boulderwood might be set up. The motion was carried, and the property purchased. Over the next six months, Board Members, excited at the prospect of sending the children to Muskoka, canvassed friends and relatives and accumulated enough money to not only pay for the property, but to undertake substantial improvements to the buildings, as well. In the meantime, preparations were well under way for Protestant Children's Homes first camping season at Boulderwood. With mounting excitement, children and staff alike prepared for the summer.

Not everyone was caught up in the camping spirit, however, or thought the rustic collection of cottages and outbuildings on the shores of Gull Lake was heaven on earth. On July 31, 1927, a somewhat hysterical telegram arrived in Toronto from Gravenhurst. It had been sent by a staff member by the name of Mrs. McKay, who declared the place "overcrowded" and possessed of "dangerous conditions – bad in every way!"

Another delegation was sent north to check on Mrs. McKay's claims. They found the place completely to their liking and cabled back to Toronto: "We are favourably impressed…by what we find and by the natural beauties of the place, the spirits and health of the children, and by the splendid work of (camp superintendent)

150 Years of Caring for Children and Families

Miss (Ida) Carr and her staff."

Mrs. McKay's concerns were not completely unfounded, however, since the minutes record that a local handyman named Goodsill was consulted regarding repairs to the "main house" in which Mrs. McKay and several little girls were staying. "My worse fears are in this crowded, ramshackle, old building," wrote Mrs. McKay in a letter that she had mailed to the chairman, Mrs. Hargraft. Goodsill recommended the bracing of a centre beam and, as a precaution, the installation of some posts beneath the room occupied by Mrs. McKay, which projected over the front verandah of the old house – apparently at an angle steep enough to have convinced the lady that she, her bedroom, and all of its contents would be deposited in the lake one night as she slept. For added safety, Mr. Goodsill suggested that ladders be leaned against two sides of the house up to the second floor, that the fire extinguishers be re-charged, and that the children be trained in fire drills.

Mrs. Hargraft was clearly annoyed by Mrs. McKay's letter, which claimed also that the main house was either going to fall down or burn down, despite the safety measures taken by Mr. Goodsill. Mrs. Hargraft told another Board Member, Mrs. McMurray, that the telegram and letter had, "created a very bad atmosphere" and that she thought Mrs. McKay should be recalled with the little girls at once. But after discussing the matter at length, the Board decided that it would not be fair to the children to deprive them of the benefits of the camp.

As for Mrs. McKay, none of Mr. Goodsill's efforts appear to have assuaged the poor woman's misgivings about Boulderwood. It is not known if she was summoned to the city on her own. But if she stayed, it is extremely doubtful that she ever surrendered to the charms of Muskoka.

Throughout the summer of 1927, and again in the summer of 1928, the Board approved numerous renovation and restoration projects around the camp. A cookhouse, sleeping porch, and external staircase were added to the main building. The cottages

Family Day Care Services

were painted and, with the help of some of the children, a rock wall was erected to protect the shoreline. In fact, one section of the wall, which was built by a boy named Kelly, came to be known as Kelly's Landing. A new cottage named after Elizabeth Busteed, who left money to the Protestant Children's Homes, was built and furnished by a grant from the Colonel George Taylor Dennison Chapter of the International Order of the Daughters of the Empire.

In one of the cottages was a large stone fireplace. A number of rustic ornaments rested on its broad mantel, including a piece of birch bark on which was written a poem by John Oxenham. The poem read:

> *"Kneel always when you light a fire.*
> *Kneel reverently,*
> *And grateful be*
> *For God's unfailing charity.*
> *And on the ascending flame inspire*
> *A little prayer which shall up bear*
> *The incense of your thankfulness*
> *For this sweet grace of warmth and light,*
> *For here again is sacrifice*
> *For your delight."*

In the summer of 1928, Miss Carr organized a field day for the children and invited the townsfolk of Gravenhurst and the summer residents of Gull Lake to inspect the camp and join in the fun. To the children's delight, the guests also provided all the prizes for the three-legged races and swimming competitions.

Sadly, the Boulderwood experience was a short-lived one for the children of the Protestant Children's Homes. In December 1929, a projected operating deficit for the coming year compelled the Board to consider closing Camp Boulderwood. The following January, representatives of the University of Toronto's Settlement House – a community-based organization that began in 1910 and

150 Years of Caring for Children and Families

which sought to provide various opportunities to underprivileged children from the city – approached the Board of Protestant Children's Homes with a proposal to rent Camp Boulderwood. When asked what she thought of the proposal, Miss Gorrie told members of the Board that none of the U.S. child care agencies she had recently visited owned or operated a summer camp. She insisted also that the agency's foster mothers were often reluctant to give up their children for part of the summer. But she appeared to contradict herself by encouraging the Board to consider sending the boys to farms for two weeks at a time, and the girls to the Canadian Girls In Training Camp. At the next Board meeting, it was agreed to rent the camp to University Settlement House for $250 per season.

Throughout the 1930s, University Settlement House continued to rent Boulderwood for its summer camping program. Mounting repair and maintenance bills and a dispute with the Town of Gravenhurst over the water level of Gull Lake ultimately persuaded the Board to sell the property. On May 28, 1940, Boulderwood was sold to University Settlement House, which kept it open until 1967, when the provincial government expropriated the land to build a highway.

Today, few cottagers who travel along Provincial Highways 35 and 121, between Miner's Bay and Haliburton, would realize they are bypassing a spot that occupies such a special place in the hearts of so many of Toronto's seniors who, when they were very young and in need of care and affection, learned to kneel and offer a prayer when they lit a fire and to trust someone else when they were frightened.

Family Day Care Services

The Universal Mother

While the Camp Boulderwood experience was short-lived for Protestant Children's Homes, the relationship that the Agency developed with its growing list of foster mothers lasted for many years. But in the initial stages, the shift from institutional to foster care compelled Protestant Children's Homes to acquaint the public with the emerging role played by the women who took up this special kind of work.

In another article that appeared in *The Globe* in the spring of 1929, Mrs. Hargraft said, "You have been hearing a great deal about foster mothers. Here you have a universal mother." This was an apt description of those women whose strong nurturing instincts and willingness to act as surrogate parents for children in need set them apart. Only after the home-finding worker satisfied herself by means of a thorough investigation that involved every member of the applicant's family were foster mothers accepted for service. Workers looked for women of compassion and upright character, who, with the help and encouragement of their husbands, offered children a stable home environment. And while foster mothers were paid, the remuneration was modest; barely more than enough to meet the basic material requirements of the foster child. Thus, any woman who might have been motivated to apply solely for monetary reasons quickly changed her mind and sought work that was far more financially rewarding.

In the spring of 1930, five months after the stock market crash that precipitated the Great Depression, monthly boarding rates paid to foster mothers ranged from $4.00 to $4.62 per week, per child, depending upon the specific needs of each child. By December of that year, both the Protestant Children's Homes and the Toronto Children's Aid Society, which also supplied foster care, agreed to set boarding rates to foster mothers at a flat $4.15 per week, per child.

From the early 1930s onward, foster mothers were invited to

The "universal mother" with three foster children.

attend lectures and seminars on home economy and child health at the Agency's Selby Street headquarters. Out of these educational sessions came the idea of establishing a Foster Mothers' Association, which afforded the women and Agency staff an opportunity to meet and discuss matters of mutual concern.

Another innovation in child care developed by the Agency in 1933 was officially called "assistance care." Also known as the foster homemaker care plan, it sought to keep motherless children with their fathers by placing a foster homemaker in families with three or more children, rather than separating the children from their fathers and placing them in foster care. In those cases that lent themselves to foster homemaking, families were given perhaps their only opportunity to stay together. Foster homemakers had to possess the same qualities as other foster mothers and be prepared to enter someone else's home and manage it as though it were her own. The Agency paid the homemaker's wages and often supplemented the father's income, as well. In the first year of the program, foster homemakers cared for 36 children in 10 households. The biggest challenge to the Agency quickly proved to be supplying the growing demand for suitable homemakers. In an era of unprecedented financial restraint, the program proved a great success, for the cost of delivering the service was exactly half of what it would have been had those 36 children been placed in foster homes.

Since the inception of foster care, Protestant Children's Homes had supplied all of the clothing that each child needed. Much of it was second hand and had been donated, but many garments had been purchased new, warehoused at Selby Street and then distributed as needed to the foster homes. In 1934, however, the Board changed its policy. Foster mothers were given a clothing allowance for each child in their care to spend as they saw fit. They quickly proved that they were shrewd shoppers, for the result was an immediate and significant saving to the Agency with no reduction in the quality or quantity of the clothing provided to the children.

In 1935, there was a move within the Federation of Community

Family Day Care Services

Services to consolidate Toronto's three child protection agencies, the Children's Aid Society, the Infants' Home, and Protestant Children's Homes. Each was asked to prepare a position paper in support of its existence as an autonomous agency. Miss Gorrie attended a Federation meeting to discuss the amalgamation of the agencies and reported to the board that the meeting was "most unsatisfactory and unpleasant." The topic was occasionally raised at Federation over the next two years, but by the spring of 1937, it had withered away.

Canada was among the nations hardest hit by the Great Depression. And while the four western provinces suffered the most during the Dirty Thirties and near crushing economic hardship had already battered the Atlantic Provinces during the 1920s, more heavily industrialized Quebec and Ontario also underwent economic strife, experiencing heavy unemployment. Moreover, the effects of the Depression were felt unevenly between classes. While falling wages and prices generated a higher standard of living for property owners and those fortunate enough to have a job, they produced the opposite effect for farmers, the young, small business proprietors, and the unemployed. As in all cases of economic and social upheaval, the families of the poor – especially the women and children – suffered the most.

An article that ran in the *Toronto Daily Star* in February 1939 highlighted the plight of many Toronto children who, according to Margaret Hall, then executive secretary of Protestant Children's Homes, lived in squalor that was "almost unbelievable."

Miss Hall told reporters who attended the Agency's annual general meeting: "We find children ragged, dirty, undernourished, and living in badly overcrowded quarters that are often not fit for human habitation."

It was not uncommon, she said, to find families of four or more living in two small, badly ventilated rooms. As had happened before, when hard times hit, applications for admission to all of the child welfare agencies increased. And the same reasons children

Deplorable housing was often the fate of Canada's impoverished children during the great depression.

150 Years of Caring for Children and Families

had come into care nearly 90 years before, when the Sullivan Street orphanage first opened, applied during the Great Depression: a mother's illness or death, the desertion by the father, or the inability of either remaining parent to adequately care for the child.

As the 1930s came to a close, rising food prices forced foster mothers to devise better ways to stretch their grocery budget and still maintain the nutritive value of the meals they prepared. A number of the children who came into care were undernourished and underweight. Restoring these children to health became a major concern. A dietitian was hired who conducted weekly lectures on nutrition for foster mothers. Every child who was taken into care received a thorough medical examination before being placed in a foster home. Once in the home, regular checkups at the Selby Street clinic followed and, because the dental hygiene of more than half the children had been overlooked completely, visits to the dentist also occurred.

Foster mothers had to be particularly sensitive to the emotional needs of the children they took in. Many of them had been neglected or abused and, as a result, had developed low self-esteem and behavioural problems. Often, they were unable to control their anger or suffered from serious eating disorders. The juvenile courts labelled some of these children "delinquent" and assigned those who were not sentenced to periods of custodial care at industrial schools, reformatories, or farm colonies, to the Children's Aid Society, which in turn placed them with Protestant Children's Homes. In this regard, the ongoing series of child psychology lectures and seminars given by members of the Protestant Children's Homes staff, and the foster mothers own association network, were very helpful and supportive.

Sadly, in the 1930s and 1940s, none of Toronto's child welfare agencies were set up to receive children with epilepsy or those children who, today, would be identified as physically challenged. The agencies reflected societal attitudes of the time and considered such children "unplaceable." Developmentally challenged children,

Family Day Care Services

whose ability to learn was then regarded as "retarded," might have been admitted to Protestant Children's Homes had there existed a way of providing to them special care and training prior to their placement in foster homes. As well, the needs of children suffering from psychiatric disorders were inadequately met. They were confined in the asylum in Orillia, or in the Mimico Reformatory. Protestant Children's Homes joined the other agencies in appealing to the Welfare Council of Toronto for special observation homes to care for them.

"We'll meet again, don't know where, don't know when…"
When war was declared in September 1939, an added strain was placed on Protestant Children's Homes because many more children came into care. Before the war, most of the children admitted to the Agency had been deprived of parental care through the illness or death of one or both parents. When the war began, however, men enlisted in the armed services while their wives, needing to bring more money into the household, took up factory work producing war materials. In the first years of the war, the number of children requiring foster care increased dramatically at a time when the number of people applying to become foster parents was declining.

In an appeal that appeared in a 1941 *Globe and Mail* article, Protestant Children's Homes head social worker, Margaret Hall, was quoted as saying, "Surely it is a part of our patriotic duty to open our doors to Canadian children, especially children of soldiers. I am sure there must be many women who would readily offer their services as foster mothers if they but knew the need."

While the appeal encouraged a number of women to apply as foster mothers, throughout the war, the shortage of good foster homes remained a serious problem.

Many foster sons joined the Canadian Armed Forces. Regardless of the fact that no blood relationship existed, their foster parents regarded them as sons nevertheless. Throughout the war members of the Foster Mothers Association met regularly to pack "comfort boxes" containing sweaters, socks, toiletries, candy and cigarettes, which they sent to their sons, wherever they were posted.

During WWII, foster mothers prepared "comfort packages" for former foster sons in the Service.

England, Wednesday, August 19, 1942

"How did that little rhyme go again?" Danny asked himself, as he and his pals jounced around the noisy, rank-smelling landing craft which was being buffeted by choppy seas and the wash of scores of other nearby boats that were part of a huge armada making its way under cover of darkness across the English Channel.

"Something like, Monday's child is full of grace…no, that ain't it. Let's see. Let's see. Monday…Monday's child is fair of face,…yeah, that's how it goes, fair of face."

Now, what was the rest of it?

Mrs. B. had taught the Mother Goose rhyme to him, patiently saying it over and over again each night before bed until he had it right. Mrs. B. and Mr. B., that's what he'd called his foster parents. Mom and Dad had somehow seemed too intimate. Besides, with two sons of their own still at home, Danny didn't feel right calling them that, though he'd often longed to.

"Monday's child is fair of face."

"My gosh," thought Danny, "that was 12 years ago." He couldn't remember the silly thing now to save his soul. In fact, he couldn't remember much at all, except what he was supposed to do when he and his buddies hit the beach about five minutes hence. For weeks, they'd practised on a near replica of the target that had been constructed in the camp where he'd been stationed. Everything, right down to the smallest enemy machinegun nest, had been duplicated. They knew the town, or at least its phony twin, almost as well as they knew the streets, back lanes, and fields they'd played in as kids.

"Tuesday's child is…full of grace. Wednesday's child…"

"Hey! Wednesday's child, that's me," thought Danny, who'd been born in Toronto on a muggy Wednesday afternoon in August exactly twenty-three years before. "And what did you get yourself for your birthday, Danny ol' boy?" he whispered to himself. "Why, I fixed myself up with a little trip to France. Pretty swell, eh?"

Rural couple who became foster parents.

150 Years of Caring for Children and Families

Wednesday's child is full of…

He stopped there and thought back to the four years he'd spent with Mr. and Mrs. B., of the big red brick house on Manning Avenue, even of the after-school paper route he'd had. But that was a long time ago, long enough to forget a nursery rhyme maybe, but not nearly long enough to forget the warmth and kindness of the woman who had taken the time each night to teach it to him. And here she was still taking time to write him letters and to send him parcels. Tucked inside the last one was a picture of her standing arm in arm with Mr. B., both of them grinning, she in her apron, he in the striped woollen trousers and shirt sleeves he always wore. Danny kept that picture inside the tin cigarette case in his breast pocket. He reached inside his tunic for it and, squinting hard in the gloom, tried to make out their faces. No use, it was too dark, and the pitching of the landing craft prevented him from holding their image still. No matter, he had it memorized.

Somebody interrupted his reverie by vomiting – no doubt a case of nerves, thought Danny. They'd be landing soon, and then all hell would break loose as each man slogged through the surf and across the killing beach, under heavy German fire, to the cover of the sea wall.

"Wednesday's child is full of…woe."

He slid the cigarette case containing the picture back into his breast pocket and grabbed his rifle.

"Happy birthday!" Danny whispered to himself. "Welcome to Dieppe."

84

Family Day Care Services

The fathers of children who were charges of Protestant Children's Homes, and who were in the armed forces, also received comfort boxes from the foster mothers. These packages carried a special cargo – photographs, cards and letters from the soldiers' children, as well as reports on their progress from their foster parents.

While the foster mothers remembered their sons who served in the war effort, many busied themselves in preparation to receive into their homes some young refugees from Europe. War Guests – children from Britain who had been sent to Canada to protect them from Nazi attack – also swelled the numbers of children who were cared for by Protestant Children's Homes. Miss Hall had taken part in a national planning conference on the care of British refugee children, which had been held in Ottawa early in June 1940. It was agreed that the federal government would be responsible for transporting the children to Canada, and that each provincial government would receive the children at special depots set up for that purpose, where they would undergo complete medical and dental examinations. The children would then be released to the various Children's Aid Societies, who would take responsibility for placing and supervising their care in approved foster homes.

Later that month, the executive committee of Protestant Children's Homes formally offered the provincial government and, by extension, the Toronto Children's Aid Society, assistance in finding suitable foster homes for the British children. To demonstrate their support for the executive committee, the entire staff of the Agency agreed to work overtime without pay to investigate homes in which to place the children. When the first block of 50 children had been placed, the Children's Aid Society asked Protestant Children's Homes to take on the added responsibility of supervising their placements, as well.

Since caseloads were already high, and because staff had voluntarily cut back on the amount of time they would take for their annual leave, the executive committee decided to hire, on a

The Agency received numerous British children who were sent to Canada during WWII to shelter them from Nazi attack. (Above photo and photo on following page.)

150 Years of Caring for Children and Families

Family Day Care Services

temporary basis, one additional caseworker, Mrs. Jean Kohl. During the months of July and August 1940, Mrs. Kohl and a team of 25 volunteer workers investigated more than 360 foster home applications.

Everyone at Protestant Children's Homes made a contribution to the British War Guest Program, including certain Board members who quietly paid the additional expenses incurred by the Agency's salaried and volunteer workers. That is why it was particularly difficult for the Agency to withdraw from the work at the end of August due to lack of funding from the Federation of Community Services, a forerunner of the United Way.

Another important initiative undertaken at about the same time by the Agency, and which would suffer the same fate as the British War Guest Program, was the Foster Day Care Program. It began as a twelve-month experiment in day nurseries in February 1940. Prior to the Protestant Children's Homes taking over the experiment, it had been a project of the Foster Day Care committee of the Victoria Crèche. The Agency agreed to conduct a pilot project to provide day care in foster homes to the children of Protestant women employed in industry, and to share the project findings with both the Jewish and Roman Catholic communities, who were interested in conducting their own foster day care programs.

The experiment got under way in March 1940 with the admission of 14 children from the Victoria Crèche, which also offered the service. By June, there were 25 children enrolled in the program, and by September there were 41. When the one-year trial was over, 58 children from 44 families had received an average of 14 days care per month. The program was an unqualified success. But to continue providing foster day care, Protestant Children's Homes depended upon further funding from the Federation. When the Federation of Community Services withheld approval for any "new" programs, citing wartime fiscal restraints, the Agency reluctantly ended the experiment. The Board's disappointment at having to abandon the program was evident in a comment made by Agency president Mrs. Lawrence Goad, who was quoted in the *Evening Telegram* of February 19, 1941 as saying, "This is a pity because the demonstration proved the need for such care, and the fact that it can be successfully given. We hope this type of service will be included in any extension of child care in Toronto."

In fact, a form of day care very similar to that delivered in the early 1940s by Protestant Children's Homes would one day be extended by the Agency to families living in and around Toronto, but not before 30 years had passed.

⁂

In January 1942, the Child Welfare Council of Toronto, of which Protestant Children's Homes was a member, sought to provide a modified form of foster day care to the children of women in industry. They made a presentation to the Minister of Public Welfare. By May of that year, legislation had been enacted that allowed the federal (Dominion) government to spend the necessary dollars to provide day care for the school-aged children of working mothers. Under the new legislation, various agencies would serve hot lunches throughout the school year to children who qualified for the program. In addition, the children would receive after school care until their mothers returned from work. The new program would be the responsibility of the Selective Service Department. In July, the federal government announced an additional program to organize day nurseries for mothers working in war industries on a national basis. It appointed women from across the country to sit as its representative on each of the provincial boards which were set up for that purpose.

In the end, only Ontario and Quebec made use of these funds to share the cost of setting up and operating a number of day nurseries. By September 1945, there were reportedly 28 day nurseries operating in Ontario, 19 of which were located in

Toronto. The cost of this program was shared equally by the Dominion and provincial governments, but it, too, came to an end. With the war over, women who had been employed in industry were discouraged from remaining in the workforce. Women who had held government jobs were actually legislated out of the workforce to make room for returning soldiers. In May 1946, the Child Welfare Council was informed that federal funding for the program would be withdrawn, and that the program would cease as of June 30. In Toronto, that meant that 1,100 children would no longer receive hot lunches and after-school supervision.

By November 1946, nine out of 28 day nurseries were closed, and the continued viability of the remaining programs was in doubt. With the withdrawal of federal support, the provincial government suggested that the Ministry of Education and local school boards assume shared responsibility for the program. The Toronto Board of Education had no money to make up the shortfall. The City of Toronto expressed an interest in continuing the program with provincial assistance, but since its 1946 budget had already been struck, any cost-sharing agreement with Queen's Park would have to wait another year. In the meantime, something had to be done.

In uncharacteristically stiff language, the Board of Protestant Children's Homes sent strongly worded letters to both the Dominion and provincial governments urging them to reconsider their decision to withdraw their financial support for day care. Within a matter of days, the Board received written replies from representatives of both governments advising that while the matter was under review, it was, after all, "a local responsibility." In 1946, the Ontario government passed the Day Nurseries Act to regulate and fund the operation of group day care centres. Such centres, which would focus on early childhood development, were believed by specialists at the University of Toronto's Institute of Child Study to be the only appropriate form of care for children in their early years. This belief was driven by the progressive education movement and by the comparatively new social science of

150 Years of Caring for Children and Families

psychology. The Institute, which was established in the 1920s, provided the model for the wartime child care centres and supplied the teachers to work in them. But the publicly-run centres were expensive to build and staff. Moreover, they were too few and far between to meet the needs of the vast majority of working mothers, who were obliged to make their own arrangements for the care of their children.

In the face of government reticence to adequately fund day care, a handful of Toronto child care agencies continued to offer various forms of day nursery care. Their varied practices and procedures came under the scrutiny of an extensive 1949 survey of family and children's services, which was conducted by a team of professional social workers from the United States, under the auspice of the Welfare Council of Toronto. In addition to making numerous recommendations aimed at both raising and standardizing the level of day care made available to Toronto families, the survey team outlined the fundamental need for such a service:

"Group day care," the authors of the report stated, "is an important and appropriate service for children whose families, for reasons of economic and social need, must seek help during part of the day for the care and supervision of their children. It is a service designed to offer full developmental opportunities to each child through participation in group living program organized according to the child's age level and interests and abilities. It is a supplement to family living. The child's ability to benefit from group day care depends largely on the parents' ability to use the service as a means of strengthening the family unit. It is not a substitute for any other service, having unique values of its own. Its use often means keeping families together. It is mental hygiene which prevents personality damage to children, resulting from inadequate care and guidance during early years."

All that may have been true, but for tens of thousands of working mothers, group day care would forever remain out of reach.

Charting a New Course, Finding a New Home

The troubled years that spanned the Great Depression and World War II placed a serious strain on the modest resources of the Protestant Children's Homes and her sister agencies throughout Toronto. Yet they were also exciting years filled with challenge, for they compelled everyone associated with the organization to examine closely the ways in which the Agency served the needs of Toronto's underprivileged children and their families, and forced them to devise new ways of meeting those needs. In the spring of 1944, the Executive Committee had appointed Jean Kohl to conduct a thorough study of the function and duties of every staff member. The result was a comprehensive report which, for the first time since the organization began offering foster care, detailed the many steps taken by Agency social workers and administrators, from the moment they received an application for admission, until a child left the organization's care.

The report was most instructive and useful for Board members because it gave them virtually an hour-by-hour account of the myriad duties performed by intake workers, home finders, case workers, and administrative staff. It engendered amongst the members of the Board a much deeper appreciation for the pressures the staff operated under, and enabled them to make informed decisions about policies and the allocation of money.

Mrs. Kohl's study also identified clearly the various sources of funding that the Agency's annual operating budget relied upon. These included fees paid by parents or other family members who were able to shoulder the full or partial maintenance costs of the children in care; an annual allotment from the Federation for Community Services; a per diem paid by the City's Welfare

150 Years of Caring for Children and Families

Trained staff was essential if foster care
were to help children as it should.

Department for the children of financially dependent families; a number of other government grants; and interest earned on various capital investments, most notably on the mortgages the Agency held on various residential properties around the city.

Finally, after years of experimentation, as well as temporary and trial programs, the report redefined the specific role of the Protestant Children's Homes amongst the city's child protection agencies.

"We are," wrote Mrs. Kohl, "a private philanthropic organization, operating as a member of the Federation for Community Services to give foster home care to children whose homes have been temporarily or permanently broken through illness or death of the mother, separation or divorce of both parents; to the unmarried mother who must work to support herself and her child, and to the child who, for reasons of health or behaviour, must be temporarily removed from his own home. Children come into care at the request of the parent, who retains guardianship and may remove him at any time."

A postwar housing shortage in Toronto, which caused many children to remain in care instead of returning home to their parents, rising divorce rates, and the admission of steadily increasing numbers of emotionally disturbed children, continued to stretch the resources of the Protestant Children's Homes to the limit. Of course, a persistent shortage of suitable foster home applicants made things even more difficult. The scarcity and comparatively high turnover of foster homes in the period immediately following the war could be blamed in part on the housing shortage. It led to uncertainty in living arrangements for many, including prospective foster parents, and an increase in the cost of living.

According to the report of the 1949 Welfare Council of Toronto survey, too few professionally trained supervisory and casework personnel worked for the seven Toronto agencies offering foster care. The report's authors claimed this represented "the greatest weakness in the child welfare field." Large caseloads

Family Day Care Services

prevented workers from properly preparing foster children and their parents for the emotional upheaval that their separation would cause. Trained staff was essential if foster care were to help the children as it should, and if the agencies hoped to reduce burnout amongst its foster parents. Moreover, there were not enough emergency care facilities capable of receiving children on a moment's notice, and too few foster parents specially trained to "cushion the shock to children who were suddenly separated from their parents."

At about the time that the survey results were released, the Children's Aid Society of Toronto and the Infants' Homes of Toronto were planning a merger. Concerned that such an amalgamation would compromise service to children and families in need, the report's authors urged the Board of Protestant Children's Homes to ensure that the Agency remained a distinctively separate organization, and that it expand its services to children of all ages throughout Greater Toronto.

By March 1946, the Agency had found itself in search of a new home. The house at 28 Selby Street, which had served the organization so well for 17 years, was no longer large enough to accommodate a growing staff and the increasing number of uses to which it had been put. For a time, the Board had considered renting and then purchasing a coach house located at 204 St. George Street, but they were never able to come to terms with the property owner. As well, a delegation had been sent to inspect the Agency's old headquarters at 229 Gerrard Street East, with a view to buying it back. However, in September 1946, the Board learned that the properties at 380 and 382 Sherbourne Street at Carlton Street were on the market and made an offer to purchase, which was at first rejected. Eventually, a price was agreed upon and the staff of Protestant Children's Homes prepared for a move to the building at 380 Sherbourne Street. It would become its headquarters for the next 54 years. The second property, a coach house at 382 Sherbourne Street, would house the Agency's caretaker.

The Agency moved to Sherbourne Street in 1947.

150 Years of Caring for Children and Families

93

The Dollhouse at 380 Sherbourne Street.

The house at 380 Sherbourne Street boasted an interesting, if somewhat shady, history. It had once been the property of local racing tout, philanthropist and man about town, Abraham Orpen, who, according to legend, kept a mistress and an illegal gambling operation on the third floor. Entrance to his little hideaway was gained through a secret passage. He was an avid horseracing fan. The deed to the property went back and forth numerous times between Orpen and various family members and acquaintances in response to the ebb and flow of his gaming fortunes. The first meeting held in the new quarters took place on May 13, 1947.

While the postwar period brought prosperity to many Torontonians, it failed to ease the hardships experienced by the inner city poor, whose already low standard of living continued its relentless downward spiral. Already beset by an appalling lack of suitable housing, poor families found that the cost of living rose far faster than their meagre incomes. Those among them fortunate enough to have had jobs earned between 38 cents and 53 cents an hour over a sixty hour, six-day week. Such exploitative wages forced many low income families to reduce their consumption of milk, meat, vegetables, and fruit, and to replace such staples with less nutritious, starchy foods. Their health was compromised by poor diet and led inevitably to a serious deterioration in their children's dental hygiene, as well.

Many Agency foster parents found themselves caught in the economic crunch as well. Some of them reluctantly withdrew their services because it had become too expensive to house, feed and clothe the children. At that time, foster parents in rural areas received $18 a month and those in the city received $20. Foster parents caring for children under four received $22 a month. To these modest pay schedules was added $4 of the $5 monthly family allowance for each child. The other dollar was held in trust to take care of any emergencies. Foster parents used to break even, but when rising prices compelled them to reach deeper and deeper into their own pockets to make up the difference, some of them decided

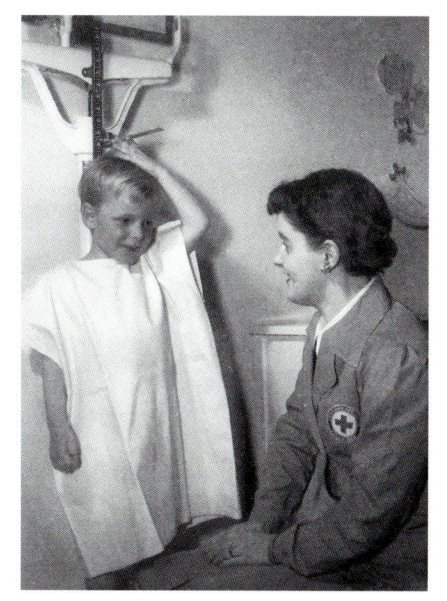

A visit to the Doctor.

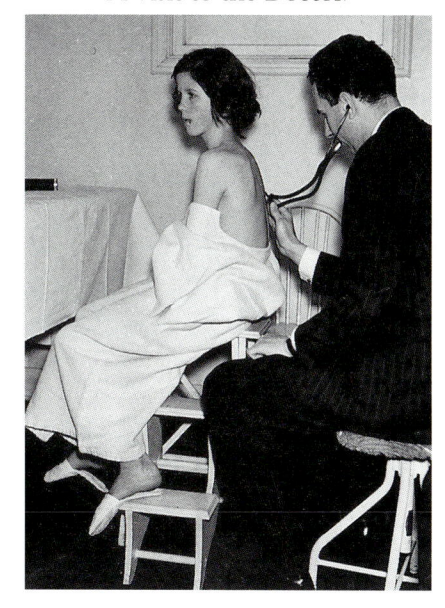

100th anniversary dinner at Casa Loma.

they'd had enough. Under such tight financial circumstances, it was difficult for the Agency to find new foster homes. Protestant Children's Homes was not in a financial position to increase payments to foster parents. Already it was hard-pressed to properly outfit each child before he or she was placed in a foster home. In 1946, the average cost of outfitting a child about to be placed in a foster home was $62.68. By 1948, the cost had jumped to $80.

At the 1949 annual general meeting of the Protestant Children's Homes, the problems of all the foster care agencies were summed up by a visiting speaker representing the Buffalo Children's Aid Society. She said increased board rates to foster parents, more public recognition of the service they provided to the community, and greater support from churches would encourage more people to apply to become foster parents. Without such support, she said, there would forever be a shortage of good foster homes.

In 1952, one year after the Agency celebrated its 100th anniversary, a coalition of foster care and child welfare agencies, which included Protestant Children's Homes, successfully petitioned the city's Board of Control for an across-the-board increase of $10 a month for foster parents. In recommending the increase, the city's finance and welfare commissioners urged the province to increase its share of foster care costs, which then amounted to no more than 25 percent.

In 1953, Canada's first metropolitan government was created, when 13 municipalities were reorganized to form the Municipality of Metropolitan Toronto. The new government was responsible for water, finance, education, public transportation and welfare. Later, police and housing were added.

Government restructuring did nothing to reduce the unemployment rate, which continued to rise until, by April 1954, 35,000 Metro Toronto men were out of work. Responding to an array of socials ills that invariably accompany hard economic times – family break-up, parental desertion, child neglect and abuse, malnutrition, and the resulting strain that is inevitably placed on

150 Years of Caring for Children and Families

child care agencies like Protestant Children's Homes – members of the Toronto Welfare Council called for an extension of unemployment insurance benefits and more federal and provincial government aid. The following month, scant relief came in the form of an amendment to the province's Charitable Institutions Act. The legislature increased grants to foster care agencies to 20 cents per child per day, or approximately six dollars a month. However, federal support for social programs in general was still paltry. Indeed, the Dominion government's efforts to protect the country's most vulnerable citizens from the bad times were so feeble that a senior spokesperson for the Canadian Tax Foundation taunted Ottawa with the label "reluctant dragon."

In February 1957, the 20 cent-per-diem provincial grant was suddenly cancelled because, said the Director of Child Welfare for Ontario, "Only children in congregate care were eligible to receive it." The announcement caught the boards of Protestant Children's Homes, Jewish Family and Child Services, and Catholic Family Services completely off guard. All three agencies had recently prepared their operating budgets for the coming year and had no opportunity to make up the unexpected shortfall. They considered making a joint appeal through the Toronto Welfare Council aimed at persuading the provincial government to postpone its decision for another year. A postponement would have given them and the United Community Fund, the organization which had, that same month, succeeded the former Community Chest, and of which they were members, time to raise sufficient funds to make up for the lost grants. It took a year, but the collective $36,000 loss to the agencies was eventually replaced by another provincial grant. Nevertheless, the need to review and upgrade rates paid to foster homes and to coax sufficient funding out of various levels of government were perennial problems that would beset all of the child care agencies for many years to come.

If the agencies had good reason to be frustrated by governmental parsimony, at least they could take heart by the enactment, in January 1955, of Ontario's Child Welfare Act. The new legislation combined the Children's Protection Act of 1893 with the Adoption Act, and the Children of Unmarried Parents Act, which were enacted in 1921. It contained improvements intended to protect children against abuse and neglect far more effectively than any preceding legislation. For the first time, adults found guilty of mistreating children were liable to a fine or imprisonment. It had taken more than a century, but at last child protection legislation had some teeth.

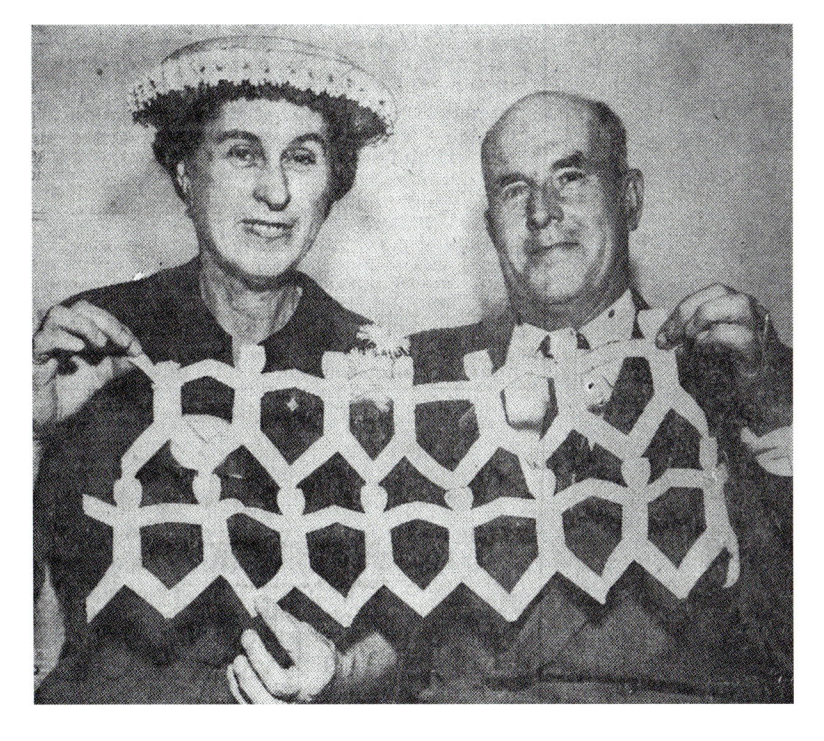

Foster parents, Mr. and Mrs. Jack Frisby, hold paper doll chain representing each of the 15 children they cared for in 26 years.

150 Years of Caring for Children and Families

Your Child

IN A FOSTER HOME

An explanation to parents

PROTESTANT CHILDREN'S HOMES
380 Sherbourne Street - Toronto

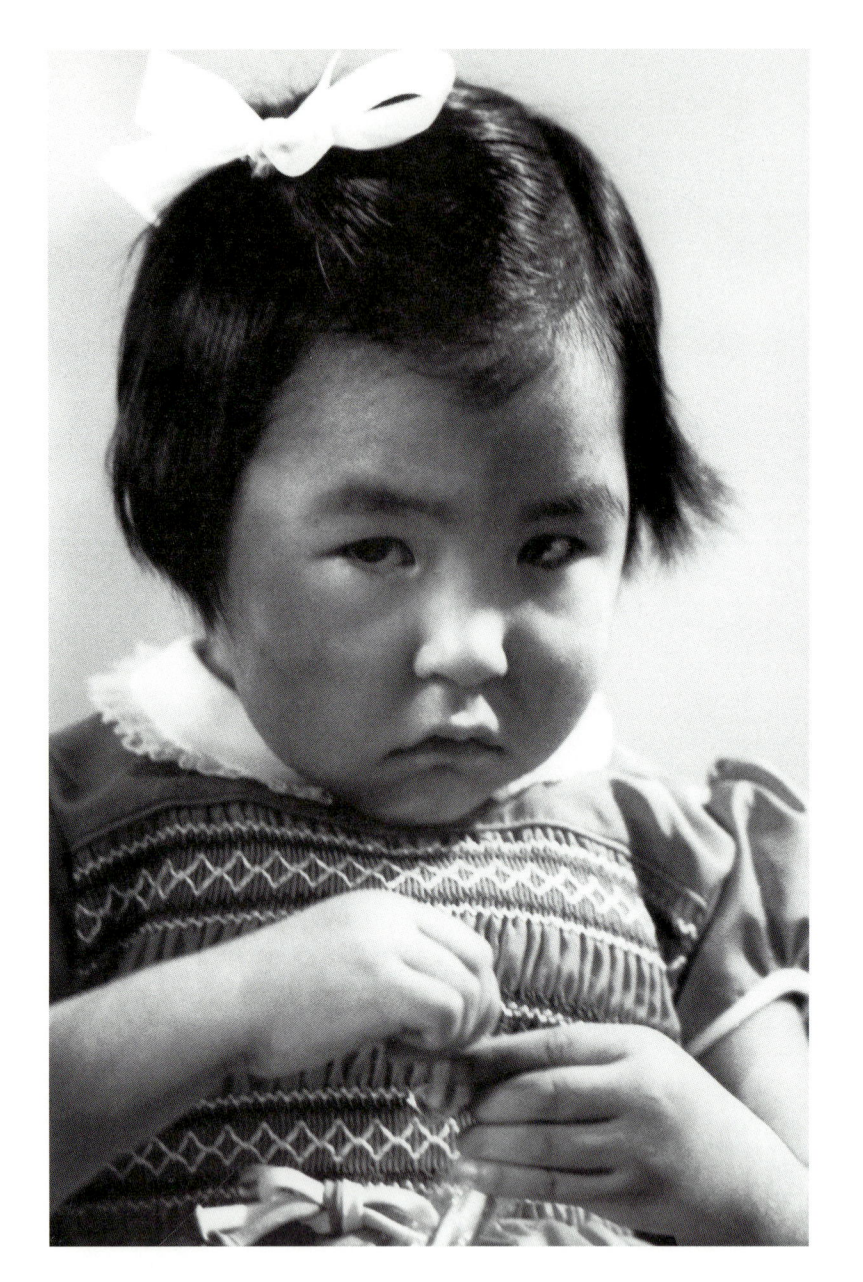

Toronto, 1968

With one tiny fist Ruth clung to Mina Walker's plaid skirt, with the other she held tight to the ear of a tattered pink bunny rabbit. While Mina fussed over the packing of Ruth's small cardboard suitcase, the little girl chanced a furtive glance over her shoulder and up into the face of the timid young Inuit woman sitting a few feet away. The young woman was Ruth's mother, Naomi. After a lengthy period of treatment and convalescence for tuberculosis at Toronto's Weston Sanatorium, Naomi and Ruth were now going home to Pangnirtung, on the Cumberland Peninsula of Baffin Island.

Though the joy she felt at witnessing the mother-daughter reunion was genuine, Mina also felt deep sorrow at the thought of having to say goodbye to Ruth. She had lived with the Walker family for the full two years that her mother had been in hospital. During that time, Mina had loved and cared for the little girl as though she had been her own. Even though Mina had talked often to Ruth about her natural mother, and about the family who waited for her to return to the Arctic, a powerful bond had formed between foster mother and child. The pain of severing that bond was something all foster mothers lived with but never quite got used to. Mina was momentarily overcome at the thought of never seeing Ruth again. She shook her head apologetically at Naomi, then turned from her packing to wipe away the tears that had begun to well up in her eyes.

By contrast, the state of Naomi's heart was unfathomable. She showed no emotion whatever. Nevertheless, she could not completely disguise her mounting anticipation and nervous impatience to embark on the long voyage home. No longer would she and her daughter be separated. In a day or two, they would be reunited with the other members of their family. Their lives would return to normal. Tentatively, Naomi murmured to Ruth in her mother tongue, but the little girl held tight to Mina's skirt and did not respond. Whatever rudimentary words she had learned as a child of three were long forgotten. She looked blankly

Family Day Care Services

at her mother then turned her head away, pretending to devote all of her attention to the stuffed rabbit.

When Ruth arrived in the Walker home as a toddler, she could speak no English. Now the bright, inquisitive five-year-old could speak no Inuktitut. Like most children, she had quickly adapted to her new, if temporary, home and to the language spoken there. There was no one with whom to speak Inuktitut, and there had been too little time for Naomi to teach her daughter to speak her native language during her weekly visits to the sanatorium.

Presently, Mina composed herself and resumed her packing. Before long, Ruth was eyeing Naomi over her shoulder again and smiling shyly. Encouraged, the young mother smiled back and withdrew a plastic tortoise shell comb from a rough canvass bag containing her belongings. With the comb, she motioned for Ruth to come closer. Cautiously, the little girl released her hold on Mina's skirt and sidled timidly over to her mother, all the while averting her eyes. She allowed Naomi to reach out with the comb and run it once through her straight, black hair.

Ruth was instantly delighted. She tucked in her chin, hunched up her shoulders, and began to giggle. "Do it again," she said coyly.

Appreciating her daughter's reaction, but unable to understand what she had said, Naomi looked enquiringly at Mina, who nodded encouragement. When, once again, Naomi ran the comb through Ruth's hair, the little girl's reticence evaporated completely. She smiled broadly and climbed confidently upon her mother's lap.

"My turn," she said.

She took the comb from Naomi and, clamping it between her teeth, cupped her mother's face in her pudgy hands. When she was satisfied with the positioning of Naomi's head, she began to comb her hair.

"Nuja," said Naomi, as she grasped a small hank of her own hair, letting it run through her fingertips.

"Nuja," repeated Ruth, taking the first step in her long voyage back to life in Pangnirtung.

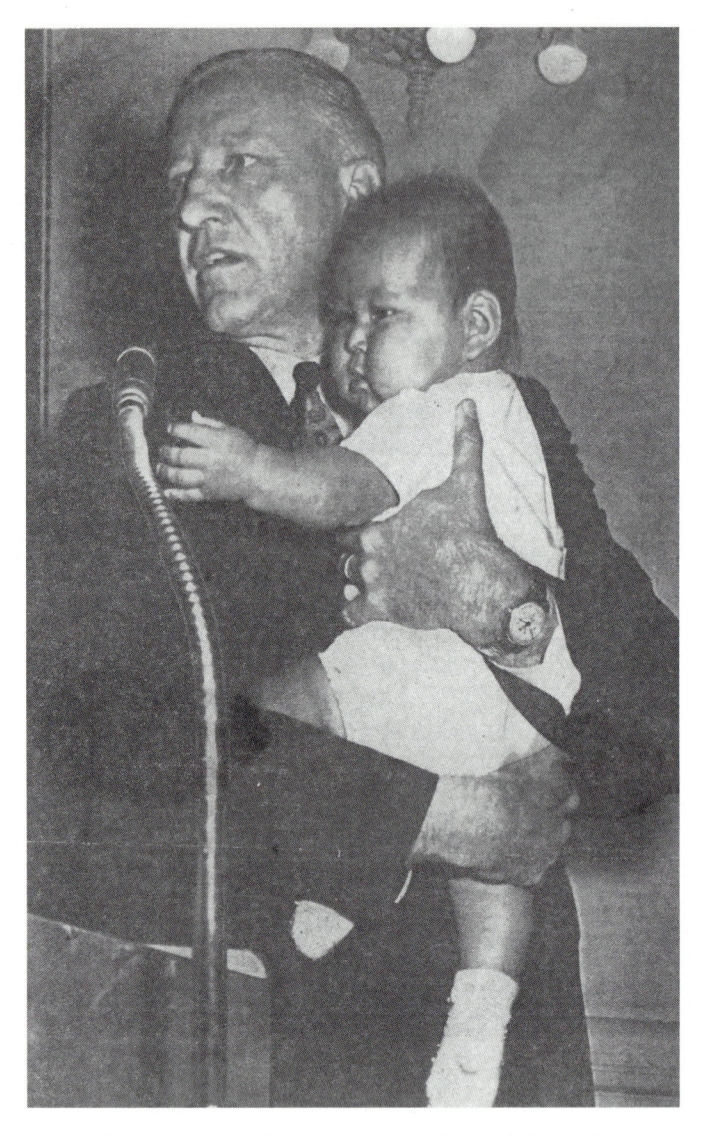

Warren Reynolds, president of Ronald-Reynolds advertising agency, holds a six month old Inuit boy.

Small Visitors from the North

In the mid-1960s, just as they had in the war years with British children, Protestant Children's Homes foster parents were called upon to shelter children from far away whose lives and those of their families were threatened by a deadly enemy. In this case, the children came from tiny Inuit settlements scattered across the vast Canadian Arctic, and the enemy was tuberculosis.

From the mid-1960s to 1970, under agreements between the child protection agencies, the Department of Indian Affairs and Northern Development, and the Department of Health and Welfare, a number of people suffering from tuberculosis were flown south were they underwent lengthy periods of treatment and convalescence at sanatoria in Montreal and Toronto. Many were mothers who refused medical attention unless at least one of their children was permitted to accompany them. Sometimes, the children themselves had contracted tuberculosis and had to be treated as well. Most times, however, the children were free of the disease and were placed in foster care until the parent had fully recovered, which, in some cases, took up to two years. Since some of the Inuit women were pregnant when they arrived, their children were born in the city. To ensure that the newborns remained healthy and free of tuberculosis, they were immediately taken into care and placed in foster homes. As a precaution, none of the Inuit children were placed in foster homes in which children 12 years or under lived.

Foster parents ensured that all of the Inuit children visited their birth parents at the Weston Sanatorium regularly. During the early stages of treatment, glass barriers separated parent and child. But as recovery progressed, they were permitted to have physical contact. And as recovery progressed still further, the birth parent was welcomed into the foster home for visits.

Foster mothers soon learned to have tea ready when the visiting mother arrived, for the Inuit woman would have done no less had she been receiving a guest in her home. They also learned that their northern visitors favoured fowl and clams, and that their musical tastes ran to gospel and country and western. A few foster mothers even ferreted out hard-to-come-by copies of an Inuit-English dictionary, which eased verbal communication, if only a little.

Nearly all of the Inuit parents feared that they would never see their children again. Protestant Children's Homes understood full well this issue of trust and prepared all of the foster parents who received the Inuit children to deal with it. Extra care was taken to make the recovering Inuit comfortable and welcome when they visited their children in the foster homes. Photographs were taken of the children and shared with their parents. Though they received plenty of love and affection from their foster families, the Inuit children were always encouraged to remember that there was another family that loved them, too, and who waited for them to return to the north.

While they were in treatment, the patients were permitted to send personal messages to family members at home via the Canadian Broadcasting Corporation's short wave Northern Service.

The Inuit foster program would continue until September 1970, when medical attention for Inuit women suffering from tuberculosis was provided by hospitals in Montreal.

150 Years of Caring for Children and Families

Protestant Children's Homes – Benefactors

Throughout its 150-year history, the Agency has relied, in part, on the generous bequests and donations of individuals whose gifts, large and small, have helped the organization maintain its high level of service to children and their families. It is impossible to list the names of every one our the Agency's several thousand benefactors, but here is a representative sample from the years between 1926 and 1971.

Caroline Adams
A.A. Allan
Robert Armstrong
Amelia Arnold
A.W. Austen
Herbert Bailey
Hanna Barnard
Francis Brawn
George Bennett
Richard Bennett
R.C. Bickerstaff
Isaac Bonner
Charlotte Boswell
Arthur Brown

John Brewer
Emma Campbell
Frances Campbell
John Carrick
John Carter
Frances Chambers
William Chalmers
Elizabeth Cawthra
Dr. William Clark
John Cowley
Harriet Crangle
Elizabeth Croft
Margaret Crownshaw
Annie Crummer

Annie Culham
Mabel Currie
Patrick Dempsey
Edwain Dennison
William Dunlop
Peter Dunn
Thomas Enright
Albert Farrance
Col. John Farewell
Agnes Fleming
Thomas Fleming
Mary Freeland
Gabriel, Daniel &
    Allen Goulter

Alison Hamilton
Mary Hargraft
Mary Haskings
Moses Henry
Edward Henry
Sampson Hogle
Mary Hogle
Ruben Holmes
Mary Howard
Katharine Howland
Katherine Hutton
Wilfred John Iredale
Edward James
continued

Family Day Care Services

Protestant Children's Homes – Benefactors

William Jennings
Robert Jessiman
Elvira Johnson
John Johnston
Samuel Johnston
Mary Johnstone
Flora Just
Sir Edward Kemp
Grace Kerr
James Kieran
James Knowles
W.H. Knowlton
Isabella Kyles
Julia Lawless
John Leckie
Charles Lockyer
William Lovering
Harriet Leak
John Low
Samuel Martin
John McColl

Walter McCosh
William McFarren
John McIntyre
Alexander McKenzie
Charles McLean
Walter McMichael
Leonard McMurray
Charles Abbs
Elizabeth MacDonald
John A. MacDonald
Sutherland Macklem
David Messenger
George Metcalfe
Pearl Moore
Peter Moore
Agnes Morrow
James Morton
Jessie McNab
Otto Niemeier
William Oke
Francis Osler

Agnes Pearce
Charles Pendrith
Agnes Penton
Edward Perkins
John Peterhaugh
William Phoenix
Rebecca Piper
Winfield Plews
Thomas Price
Mary McLachlan
Margaret Reeve
William Robinson
Francis Richardson
Francis Riddell
John Roberts
Thomas Robson
George Rogers
Dr. Albert Rolph
William Rolling
Mary Sampson
Alexander Schofield

Thomas Semple
James Shields
Douglas Taylor
Elizabeth Van der Smissen
Robert and Agnes Smith
Agnes Smith
D.M.P. Squires
Gerard Strathy
David Walton
Bessie Walton
Florence Ward
William Warren
Joseph Whealy
Elaine White
Thomas White
Thomas Woodbridge
Martha Wright
Jemima Whichelo

150 Years of Caring for Children and Families

The Challenge of Change

In March 1963, at a meeting of the East York Social Planning Council, which was attended by representatives of various social agencies and the municipal councillors of Scarborough and East York, there was general agreement that day care was a service that a rapidly increasing number of Metro Toronto families desperately needed. Protestant Children's Homes was strongly encouraged to develop a pilot day care project. When this was conveyed to the Protestant Children's Homes Board, Director of Social Work, Betty Quiggin, was asked to make preparations to conduct a pilot project.

Over the next six months, while the Day Care Committee of the East York Social Planning Council conducted a detailed needs assessment for day care amongst its clientele, Betty Quiggin examined the way in which services were delivered to the Agency's clientele. She found that between 10 and 15 percent of applications resulted in admission of the children to foster care – a comparatively small percentage. As for the remaining 85 to 95 percent of applications, the Agency helped those families to make other suitable arrangements. The evidence was clear to Betty Quiggin: Protestant Children's Homes should provide a variety of services and facilities for helping children in their own homes, not just foster care. With so many mothers entering the paid workforce in the 1960s – two of every five women working outside of the home had children – it was essential to provide a range of services, and that surely included adequate day care. Miss Quiggin told her Board that as far as she was concerned, day care was as essential to the health and well-being of society as were public utilities like water and electricity.

In September, the Board moved to go ahead with a pilot project in East York. Staff from Protestant Children's Homes worked with representatives from the Toronto Social Planning Council, Victoria

Day Nursery and St. Christopher House to develop a pilot project to test the feasibility of offering day care services in neighbourhood homes. While each agency followed guidelines set out by the Child Welfare League of America, they nevertheless developed different approaches to offering services as a way of testing this new form of day care. The following month, Miss Quiggin met again with the East York Social Planning Council and outlined her vision for her agency's part of the program. She told them Protestant Children's Homes would provide day care in supervised private homes for pre-school children, and that the cost of the program would be born entirely by the Agency, which would continue to provide foster home placement service to the children of families who needed it.

By early December 1963, the first children were received into the East York program. Within a few months, their numbers grew, and by the fall of 1965, more than 50 children were receiving day care. The program was an unqualified success, and the Agency had to appeal for secondhand playpens, highchairs, tricycles, and toys to fill the growing demand.

In October 1965, Betty Quiggin was invited to make a presentation supporting a request for more than $25,000 in program funding to the East York Township Health and Welfare Committee. Keenly interested in the program's success, and determined that it should grow, the East York Committee recommended to the Township's Finance Committee that township council approve the funding. At the same time, the Committee appealed to the Minister of Public Welfare to amend the Day Nurseries Act so that the province would share the cost of providing family day care equally with municipalities. As the law stood, the province was only obliged to share the cost of government-run day nurseries. The appeal fell on deaf ears at Queen's Park, however, and proved to be the first round in an ongoing and very public battle over funding that was waged by non-government child care agencies against the provincial government.

Working through umbrella organizations such as the Ontario

150 Years of Caring for Children and Families

Welfare Council and the Association of Women Electors, and by advocating on their own behalf, Protestant Children's Homes, Cradleship Crèche, Victoria Day Care Services, and the West End Crèche – known as the Group of Four – repeatedly petitioned the provincial government to broaden the Day Nurseries Act to recognize family day care as a complementary service to the care offered by nurseries.

In January 1966, a new Child Welfare Act came into force, which also excluded the Group of Four from shared provincial-municipal funding for their programs. Unlike wards of the Children's Aid, the children they served came into care on a voluntary basis. Under the new legislation, municipalities could not share with the province their portion of the costs to deliver foster care that was supplied by the four "voluntary" Metropolitan Toronto agencies.

In 1966, the federal government passed Canada's first national welfare legislation, the Canada Assistance Plan, which consolidated the Unemployment Assistance Plan and legislation that provided social assistance to people who were physically challenged. Incorporated within it was a cost-sharing arrangement with the provinces to subsidize the provision of day care to low income families in need, people who were so poor, they couldn't possibly pay for day care themselves, and as a preventive measure, those who were considered "likely to be in need."

In Ontario, responsibility for implementing the Canada Assistance Plan would be shared by both the provincial and municipal governments. In most other provinces, child care remained solely a provincial responsibility. Anticipating this, the Association of Women Electors, which represented 20 social agencies, including Protestant Children's Homes, took the lead in pressing Metro Council to ensure that the delivery of welfare services to area families would not suffer under the new régime.

Protestant Children's Homes was particularly worried that money which had been allotted by East York Township Council to run the family day care program there would disappear once the Metropolitan government took over. Miss Quiggin pressed Metro Council to give a definitive statement in respect of the new legislation and its likely impact on the future of voluntary day nurseries within the city. She wanted to know if there would be cost sharing for such programs between the province and Metro.

These were uncertain times for the Agency. The new Child Welfare Act transferred responsibility for many foster care arrangements to the Children's Aid and compelled Protestant Children's Homes to re-evaluate the provision of foster care. By the end of 1966, only 20 children remained in Agency foster homes. There were, however, between 60 and 70 children enrolled in the East York family day care program, and plans were underway to place 20 more in homes in North York. To further complicate matters, the United Community Fund had reduced Protestant Children's Homes funding allocation for 1966 because Metro Chairman William Allen and Welfare Commissioner John Anderson had announced that Metro intended to put more money into day care centres, then the municipality's focus, despite advice to the contrary offered by their constituents and numerous social agencies.

A notation in the Agency's minute book for May 10, 1966 reveals the Board's mounting frustration with Metro's decision:

"Recent articles in the press have made it clear that Metro Chairman Allen, and public welfare officials have been unreceptive to advice from the Social Planning Council and private agencies. There is considerable concern being voiced in the community from individuals and groups such as the Association of Women Electors."

Despite the atmosphere of uncertainty created by new legislation and the obduracy of certain local politicians and bureaucrats, the members of the Protestant Children's Homes Board remained optimistic about the future of the Agency. However, they also realized that a fundamental change in direction was required if the organization were to survive and continue to serve Toronto's needy families, as it had for the previous 115 years.

Their willingness to embrace change and their confidence that they would ultimately succeed was reflected in the minutes taken at the May 24, 1966 meeting:

"Several members ... stated that there appears to be a great future in day care for Protestant Children's Homes. Recognition was given to the problems of financing the service, but it was felt that this would resolve itself as more recognition is gained for the need of (sic) increased day care, and that P.C.H. should move forward with confidence."

A motion to realign the Agency's services by phasing out full time foster care and using the freed-up funds to develop a network of day care homes throughout the city was carried. The decision was a momentous one. Not since 1926, when the Agency decided to phase out the orphanage in favour of foster care, had such a fundamental shift in focus been made.

Having charted a new course, and realizing that success depended in large measure upon greater public awareness of the contribution family day care was making in the lives of the families who had come to rely on it, the Board decided to mount a major public relations campaign to seek support. Retaining the services of a professional public relations consultant, they focused on politicians and other community opinion-makers to help get their message out. For greater impact, the public relations launch was timed to coincide with the fall United Appeal campaign, preparations for the 1967 Metro Toronto budget, and the inauguration of the Agency's second family day care program in North York. Community leaders, such as East York Reeve True Davidson, also waded into the controversy, which the media dubbed "the crisis in day care."

"The crisis," said Davidson, "is the refusal of Queen's Park to give financial assistance to day care." At the time, the province subsidized only municipally-run day nurseries.

The Agency's Director of Child Care Services, Kathleen Sutherton, agreed with the Reeve of East York. While sitting as

Protestant Children's Homes representative on a child day care panel that was convened by the Agency in the fall of 1966, Miss Sutherton said that since 1961 there had been a sharp increase in the demand for care for babies and school-aged children of single, widowed, separated, and divorced working mothers. These women had to work to feed and clothe their children. Many believed their only option was to place their children into foster care because no alternative existed.

"The separation of a child from his or her parents just for economic reasons is a very serious experience in the life of a young child," Sutherton told reporters covering the panel discussions.

Protestant Children's Homes workers, whose clients faced such a dilemma, realized an alternative existed to full time foster care, a way to permit the mother to continue to earn a living outside the home and keep her family together. That way was some form of day care. This realization, and the agency's leadership and participation in the pilot project with the Social Planning Council and other agencies, led to the establishment of the East York family day care program. Their approach to family day care was an extension of the foster care model. It saw quality care being achieved by a thorough initial assessment of providers' home settings and families' needs, careful matching of children and providers, regular visits to providers to monitor the care they offered, and meetings with parents to ensure their ongoing satisfaction with care.

By June 1966, Metro Toronto had nine public nurseries, five United Appeal nurseries, nine church-sponsored or other non-profit nurseries, thirty private profit-making nurseries, and an unknown number of independent day care providers who were not subject to any supervision or standards whatever – a seemingly sizeable network. Even with all of these, however, the growing demand for day care far outstripped the supply.

Vast numbers of women with children had to find work outside their homes to supplement their families' incomes, even when that meant, as it inevitably did, that they received low wages. Just as child-rearing had always been undervalued by society, so was the contribution to the economy of working mothers. In one newspaper article published in 1967, Betty Quiggin wondered out loud about what would happen if women abruptly stopped working.

"It would be the same as a general strike," she said.

At the time, it had been estimated that 94 percent of stenographers, sales clerks, teachers, and nurses were women. The Ontario Ministry of Labour predicted that by 1970, women would perform 57 percent of all service industry jobs. If, to underscore their true value to the economy, these women had all decided to withdraw their services for a time, the country would have instantly suffered a crippling labour shortage, the economy would have screeched to a stop, and the overall standard of living would have plummeted. If, however, politicians and the leaders of industry and commerce were to have placed a fair value on women's contribution to the economy, and if they had acknowledged the profound importance of raising children, they would have provided affordable day care. But they didn't. And as a result, the overwhelming majority of Metro Toronto's working mothers were obliged to leave their children with relatives, neighbours, or with an unsupervised babysitter. Many had no choice but to leave their school-aged children unattended, giving rise to the term "latch key kids." Rather than jeopardize their children's safety and the unity of the family, some women left the workforce and turned to welfare. But in doing so, they often found themselves ghettoized and scorned.

Day care centres met the child care needs of some working mothers, but there were far too few centres and the municipality couldn't build them fast enough to keep up with demand. Family day care, which involved the placing of children in homes supervised by a social agency like Protestant Children's Homes, presented a better solution. The day care homes, which were obliged to meet basic health and safety standards, were often located within a short walking distance of the child's home. Because there were no high labour costs, no money had to be spent on bricks and mortar, and parents paid only what they could afford for the service, family day care was also less costly.

Most of the working mothers whose children were part of the East York program earned between $40 and $60 per week, while most of their husbands earned between $60 and $100 per week. They lived in rooms, flats, small apartments, or with relatives. On average, they paid $1.20 per day for each child's care. The actual cost for Protestant Children's Homes to screen applicants, supervise the children, administer the program, and pay the day care mothers was $4.60 per day per child.

The day care mothers, as they were called at the time, were paid $2.42 per day per child. Usually, they were women with children of their own, or women whose families had grown and left home. They were experienced in caring for children, a fact that working mothers found reassuring.

A great deal of effort went into finding suitable day care homes. In the case of one family whose working mother sought care for her three children, caseworkers searched the family's neighbourhood for a month, logging 65 kilometers on the Agency car, before a prospective day care home was found. There followed a series of pre-placement visits, medical examinations for all the children, and a chest X-ray for the day care mother, before the children spent a single day in care.

Despite the obvious need for day care and the success of the East York program, as 1967 came to a close, the Agency was deeply concerned about the future. Metro Toronto Welfare Commissioner John Anderson had recommended that no financial support be given to the program beyond 1968 because it was not eligible for provincial cost sharing. Anderson's recommendation came in for immediate criticism by East York Reeve True Davidson, who told reporters, "This is just what we were afraid of when Metro took over welfare. It is a disgusting betrayal of all the principles we were assured would be upheld. To me, the thought of dropping this service is completely improper."

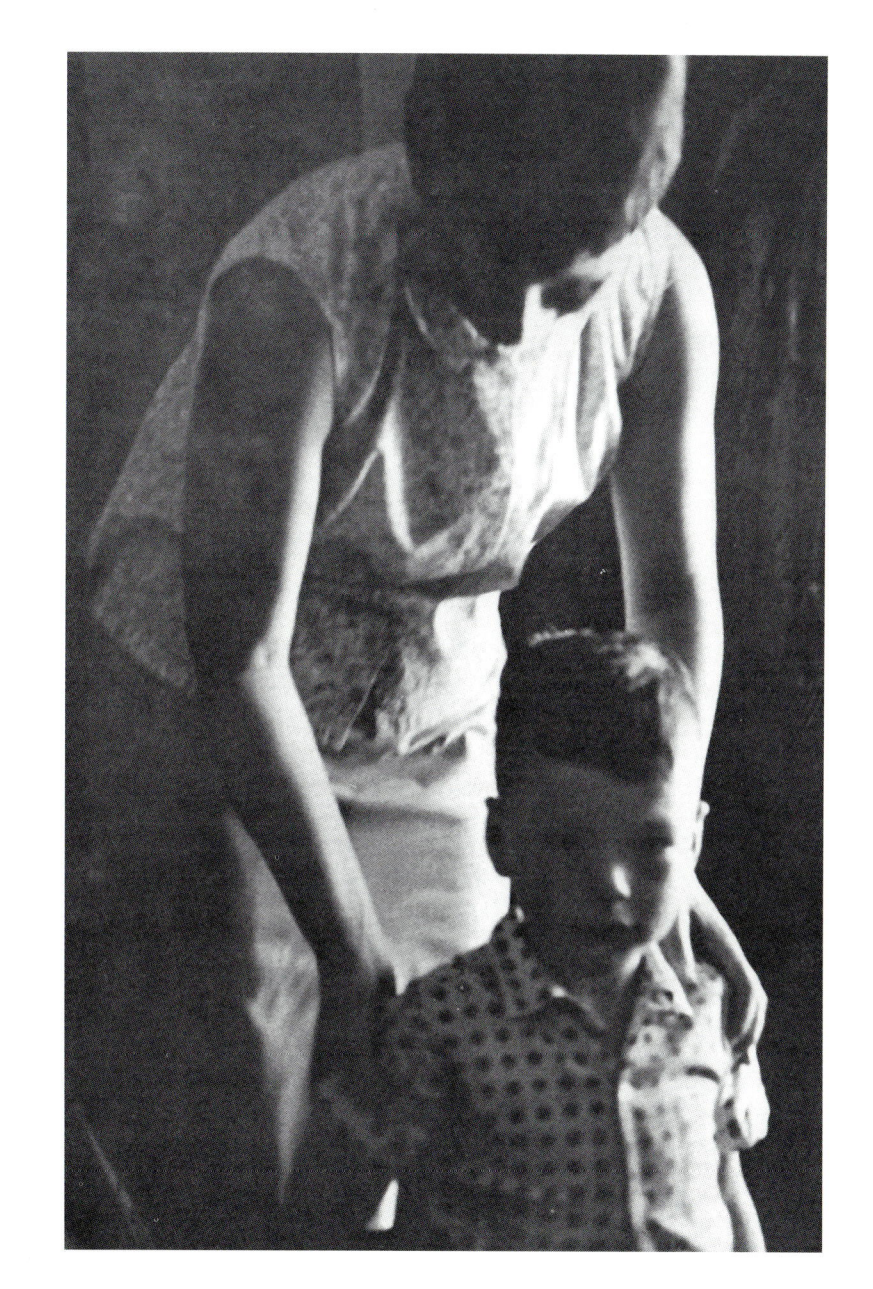

150 Years of Caring for Children and Families

Tuesday, September 17, 1968

We need a lot more day care centres

A Metro Social Planning Council report has shown that government must provide more help for the thousands of Toronto mothers who must work to support their children.

The figures are alarming: 16,924 children of working mothers are inadequately cared for; only 3,000 children are in day care centres, mainly because the centres are too few and generally too costly; some 24,000 mothers are the sole support of their children.

day while their mothers work. Or else they are passed from relative to relative or neighbor to neighbor, giving rise to emotional problems and feelings of insecurity.

There is no point in admonishing working mothers to stay home and look after their children. Many of them have no choice but to work.

Yet some governmental policies almost seem designed to make it im-

Metro to ask Ontario funds for day care

Metro welfare committee will ask the provincial Government for subsidies to operate family day-care services.

The committee endorsed a report from Welfare Commissioner John Anderson which warns that a budget allotment of $60,000 for support of day-care programs in Metro will run out in November. The money is used to assist the Protestant Children's Homes' day-care program in East York.

Mr. Anderson recommended that Metro join the Protestant

Globe and Mail, October 18, 1968

Metro Councillor and Municipal Controller Margaret Campbell, herself a working mother and grandmother, supported Davidson. "We were assured that Metro would maintain the services existing in each of the municipalities (that compose Metro Toronto)," she said, in an article that appeared in the *Toronto Star*.

In September 1968, the Metro Toronto Social Planning Council made a public appeal to government on behalf of working mothers. The Council said 24,000 women were the sole supporters of their families, and that there were 3,000 children of working mothers enrolled in Metro's day care centres. Another 17,000 children were in private arrangements. A large number of children ranging in age from six to eight years had no supervision whatever while their mothers worked. As a result, many were frightened, insecure, and had developed serious emotional problems. Their mothers were caught between the need to provide for them and government policies that made it impossible for them to get affordable and accessible day care.

While the public battle raged on, members of Protestant Children's Homes Program Committee quietly visited as many Metro area day care centres as they could in an effort to understand how they ran and the program and facilities they offered. When they had completed their survey, they made their report to the Board.

September 1968 was a pivotal time for the Agency, as was noted in the minutes of a meeting held on September 24:

"…1969 will be a crucial year as Metro has clearly stated it will withdraw its support from our program at the end of 1968 if by that time it is not covered by provincial legislation, and this seems most unlikely to us.

"The question the Executive Committee faced (and which was, at that very moment, facing the Board) was, "Are we committed to maintaining our present day care program in East York and North York, and to developing a demonstration project in group day care homes, to the extent that we are prepared to finance it from our own capital funds throughout 1969, if necessary? If we choose to assume a leadership role in the community in the development of adequate day care services, it will mean a staff recruitment and development program and a commitment to competitive salary scales for professional staff."

The members of the Executive Committee reminded the Board that they had found themselves in a similar position five years before when the Agency decided to phase out foster care in favour of family day care. At that time, the Board was prepared to underwrite the new venture. But did they have the confidence to keep the service going? The answer was a resounding and unanimous yes. Wise investments and the faith of countless individuals over the years, who donated both large and small sums of money, ensured that the Agency was in a strong enough financial position to both maintain its current programs in East York and North York and undertake a pilot project in group day care when the time was right.

In January 1969, the Agency enlisted the help of the general public by encouraging people to write to their members of provincial parliament urging them to support a change to the Day Nurseries Act that would permit funding of subsidies to families using family day care. Letters from members of the Agency's executive committee to Social and Family Services Minister John Yaremko had failed to bring about the desired result. Betty Quiggin was barely able to disguise her frustration with the government's intransigence, as the minutes of the March 25, 1969 meeting reveal:

"Miss Quiggin commented on the correspondence received from members of parliament in response to letters requesting the inclusion of family day care under the Day Nurseries Act. She noted that if we were naïve enough to think that by writing letters of explanation we could win support for this form of day care, we have learned from the replies that this is not so. The replies which have been received show an increasingly firm position which excludes not only the program, but by implication, rejects the need for it. She noted that our concern should be focused in two areas:

Editorial, Toronto Star April 7, 1969

A place for kids

> Perhaps the most telling weakness of the Ontario government is that it does not comprehend the realities of life in Metro Toronto and the other growing cities of this predominantly urban province. This has been demonstrated once again in the attitude it is taking to the difficulties of working mothers and their children.

The Telegram, March 31, 1969

Tory MPPs ignore daycare – agency

Toronto Daily Star, May 20, 1971

"Concern for the narrow and inflexible position of the Day Nurseries legislation, which continues to state that only group care is acceptable day care, and implies that every child requiring day care can best be served in a day nursery setting.

"For the unwillingness of the Department of Social and Family Services to recognize its responsibilities and its opportunities in the area of preventive and supportive services such as we are providing to the families using our day care."

Protestant Children's Homes was by no means the only agency encountering difficulties in dealing with senior levels of government. Virtually all of the delegates attending a two-day discussion on the Purchase of Services under the Canada Assistance Plan, which was sponsored by the Canadian Welfare Council, voiced the same complaint. Voluntary agencies, such as Protestant Children's Homes, felt they had no collective voice and no established channels for communicating with the government and its agencies. Neither was there any dispute resolution mechanism in place to deal with problems when they arose. There was growing fear among delegates that the Ontario government was moving inexorably towards the provision of all services under its own jurisdiction.

The future of the private, voluntary agencies was very much in question. What services would they be permitted to offer? And was there any reason to hope that they could one day look forward to provincial funding, or at least a more amenable legislative framework? Protestant Children's Homes had obviously been pondering such questions, especially the members of the Agency's Change of Name Committee. In the spring of 1969, in their attempt to describe more accurately what Protestant Children's Homes had to offer the community, the committee had narrowed down their choices to: Care and Counseling Services, Child and Family Services, Child Care and Counseling Services and, perhaps attempting to reflect the upbeat tenor of the times, Child Services Unlimited.

Family Day Care Services

In April 1969, Metro Toronto Welfare Commissioner John Anderson announced that the municipality intended to build a group day care centre in East York for the families served by the Protestant Children's Homes family day care program. Because the province would not underwrite the cost of building a new facility, the municipality intended to renovate an existing one. But since it wouldn't be ready until some time in 1970, the Agency's East York program would be permitted to operate.

When Betty Quiggin told Anderson that Protestant Children's Homes was interested in developing a group day care centre that would be eligible for provincial funding and would not call for building or even renovation costs because it would be located in a private home, he claimed such a scheme would likely run counter to municipal zoning regulations. But he did offer a ray of hope by indicating that the province had been encouraging Metro to purchase day care services from private and commercial operators, especially agencies supported by the United Appeal, like Protestant Children's Homes. Unfortunately, it was only the slimmest ray of hope, for when Anderson met with members of the Ontario Cabinet, as a representative of the Ontario Municipal Board presenting a recommendation for family day care services, he was flatly told that the government would not consider supporting family day care in any way, only group day care centres.

Also in the spring of 1969, the Agency undertook a study of group day care centres in Houston, Texas. In the early 1950s, several child care centres in that city had amalgamated to form the Houston Day Care Association. In addition to operating seven centres, each of which could accommodate between 30 and 100 children, the Association supervised 195 family day care homes. They told Protestant Children's Homes representatives that the group day care centres had ongoing problems with staff turnover, zoning and fire regulations, and health. When those who had conducted the survey returned and made their report to the Group Day Care Home Committee, it was recommended to the Board that

Toronto Daily Star, March 21, 1970

135,000 Metro children need day care help

150 Years of Caring for Children and Families

all further investigations into such a program cease, and that the Protestant Children's Homes concentrate all of its resources on family day care.

In October, Protestant Children's Homes and Victoria Day Care Services – the only agencies then offering family day care services to Metro residents – were surprised to learn that the province's Day Nurseries Branch had authorized Metro Toronto to develop and operate their own family day care project to serve 850 sole-support families in the city's west end. The private agencies received the news with some ambivalence. While they were encouraged by the provincial government's apparent, if belated, acceptance of family day care services, they were annoyed by the fact that neither of them had been consulted or even informed of the project.

The following month, Betty Quiggin met again with John Anderson and was heartened to learn that the welfare commissioner had included estimates in his 1970 budget for both the Agency's East York and North York programs. Moreover, he told Miss Quiggin that he sensed a softening in the attitudes of both Metro's Welfare Committee and the provincial government on family day care. He said that if Protestant Children's Homes maintained its high standard of care, he would recommend to his committee that the municipality increase its financial support of family day care.

In the spring of 1971, the Executive Committee placed before the Board a new name for the 120-year-old Agency, a name that won immediate approval. The change required an amendment to the Protestant Children's Homes Act in the form of a private member's bill, and on June 17, 1971, the Agency's name was changed to Family Day Care Services.

Toronto Daily Star, January 12, 1971

Ontario considers paying for day care in private homes

John Yaremko, Ontario's minister of social and family services, told working mothers last night his department is giving top priority to subsidized children's day care services.

His officials are even considering the possibility of helping to pay for day care in private homes, where a woman who stays at home looks after children of working mothers.

far short of what's needed, he told about 500 people at a Star Forum in the St. Lawrence Centre Town Hall he'd welcome pressure from municipalities with day care plans.

"Get after your mayors and your aldermen," Yaremko said, brandishing a copy of the provincial Day Nurseries Act. "The legislation is here."

The Star's 13th Forum brought the public

today's key issues: "How far should we go with day care?"

Other panelists were Mrs. Betty Bowskill, director of the Scarborough Information Centre; Mayor True Davidson of East York; John Anderson, Metro's welfare commissioner; and Professor Lorenne Smith, a prime mover of a co-operative day nursery at the University of Toronto. Moderator was Fred Hotson, manager of

Yaremko's 1970-71 budget to pay 80 per cent of day care costs across the province is $3,250,000. It would take $150 million to subsidize services for 100,000 children in Metro alone.

But Yaremko noted that the province spends more than 13 times as much on day care as it did 10 years ago and declared that "I am personally committed to a full development of day care services,

For the first time, he relaxed his department's position that the only such services worthy of subsidies are licensed groups such as day nurseries run or controlled by municipalities.

Yaremko revealed that officials have been "kicking around" the idea of combining the best elements of these group services and a family day care system,

cared for by another woman who stays at home.

He was replying to Joan Rogers, chairman of the Social Planning Council's Community Day Care Committee, who asked for a subsidy for family day care similar to the one now given group day care.

At present, the province, through a cost-sharing arrangement with the federal

150 Years of Caring for Children and Families

Family Day Care Services

1971–2001

Family Day

Toronto, 1970

It was rush hour. The breathless city air was close and sour. To the south, high above the lake, towering thunderheads threatened rain. Dorothy hoped she could make it to Christine's house on Cosburn Avenue in time to pick up her two kids and walk with them the three blocks to their tiny flat on Sammon Avenue before the heavens opened and they all got drenched.

As usual, there was standing room only on the O'Connor Drive bus when it hissed to a stop at the corner of Bermondsey Road, where Dorothy stood amidst the homeward-bound women and men who worked in the small factories that lined the nearby streets. It was the same tired group every evening – the men with their tin lunchboxes and rolled up newspapers, the women clutching purses and the occasional plastic tub that had contained a lunchtime sandwich. Though they usually nodded a perfunctory greeting each evening, they seldom spoke, and then only about the weather or some other inconsequential matter that involved no real commitment beyond the verbal shorthand that so often serves as conversation between people who are lost in their own thoughts and don't wish to be disturbed.

As the crammed bus rolled down O'Connor, lurching to a stop every few blocks to pick up and let off passengers, Dorothy thought about the evening to come. It would be a carbon copy of most other weekday evenings. If traffic weren't too bad, she'd arrive at Christine's in another twenty minutes. As they did each evening, four-year-old Michael and three-year-old Emily would greet her at the front door with something they'd made that day – a picture, maybe a Plasticine figure. Christine would faithfully give an account of everything the children had done since 7:30 that morning, when Dorothy had dropped them off on her way to work. As she talked, Christine would scurry around her livingroom and kitchen in search of stray sweaters, hats, or toys, before giving the kids a quick goodbye kiss. With a small, trusting hand in each of hers, Dorothy would walk with her children along Cosburn and down Pape Avenue to Sammon Avenue.

As Dorothy approached Christine's, she thought about how her life and the lives of her children had at last settled into a reassuring routine,

150 Years of Caring for Children and Families

123

but it hadn't always been so. Her husband, Don, had been killed in a traffic accident eighteen months before, leaving her and the children with very little money, forcing them out of their small east-end bungalow, and plunging the young mother into a deep depression. For a few months, she and the kids lived with a kindly retired couple who attended their church. They didn't ask her for room or board, but Dorothy knew her family's presence placed a financial strain on her benefactors that was proving too much for the man's modest pension. Her mother and father, who were back in Newfoundland, sent what money they could, which wasn't much. Though she had not yet taken time to grieve Don's death, Dorothy knew she'd have to get a job. But what was she going to do with Michael and Emily? She couldn't ask the elderly couple to look after them. She had no close friends nearby who could mind them while she worked. There was only a handful of day care centres scattered across the entire city and they were already full. At the local supermarket, she had seen dozens of notices placed there by working women desperate to find someone to look after their children. The headlines in the papers said over a hundred thousand Metro Toronto children were in need of day care. Even if Dorothy posted such a notice and was fortunate enough to find a woman willing to take her children, Dorothy knew she could never afford to pay her. She was in a hopeless situation, needing to provide for herself and her children, but unable to pay the full cost of day care herself.

Everything seemed to be working against her until one Sunday, when she saw a notice on the church bulletin board advertising a family day care service run by Protestant Children's Homes in East York. She jotted down the information and called the next day. Before the week was out, she had met with a social worker from the Agency who eventually introduced Dorothy and her children to Christine, who had cared for the children of other working mothers in the past and was the mother of two school-aged children herself. Dorothy liked Christine, and so did the children. An agreement was struck and the following week, when Dorothy started her job, she knew her children would have a safe, friendly place to go.

As Dorothy walked up the steps to Christine's front door, Michael popped his head out and shouted, "Hi, Mommy! Wanna see what we did today?"

Tired as she was, Dorothy knew there was nothing in the world she would rather do.

By the time Protestant Children's Homes changed its name to Family Day Care Services, the Agency's third model of child care and family support was well established. The first model was orphanage care between 1851 and 1930, and the second was foster care, which roughly coincided with the 45-year period between 1926 and 1971 (although a few older teens would remain in foster care until the late 1970s). Day care, as the Agency's new name clearly delineated, represented the third paradigm of child care to be provided by the organization.

In April 1971, three of the original group of four agencies providing child care to Toronto families – Victoria Day Care Services, Cradleship Creche, and Family Day Care Services renewed their alliance, which they dubbed the Group of Three. They and a number of other agencies concerned with the welfare of children continued to press the provincial government for amendments to the Day Nurseries Act. At times, the pressure rankled officials in the province's Day Nurseries Branch, as the following excerpt from the Agency's minutes for June 15, 1971 clearly indicates:

"Relative to the proposal that ways be found to bring pressure on Queen's Park, reference was made to the article in the *Globe and Mail* on Thursday June 10, headed 'Government Said Dragging Feet on Bringing in Family Day Care. Miss Quiggin reported that she had been contacted by a writer from the *Globe and Mail* asking for comment on **a** resolution from the Catholic Women's League. The resolution urged the provincial government and the Minister of Social and Family Services to amend the Day Nurseries Act and regulations to allow sponsoring social agencies to be eligible to receive a subsidy from public funds to set up family day care services, and quotes Protestant Children's Homes (whose name would officially be changed one week later) as having operated such a pilot project for seven years. The day the article appeared in the press, Miss Quiggin received a call from a member of the staff of the Day Nurseries Branch stating that the Director of the Branch was concerned about this article and wanted to know why the term 'illegal' had been used to describe this agency's program.

Explanation had been made that the term 'illegal' had not been used, but that this was a misquote of a comment about the lack of licensing and standards for family day care. The significance of the article and the telephone call from the Day Nurseries Branch is an indication that critical comment concerning lack of action by the provincial government is being heard at Queen's Park."

On June 15, 1971 a letter signed by the executive directors of each board of the Group of Three, requesting a meeting to discuss amendments to the Act with Thomas Wells, the Minister of Social and Family Services, was delivered to Queen's Park. Coincidentally, the first National Conference on Day Care was to be held in Ottawa the following week, a fact that ensured public attention would remain focused on the difficulties Canadian families had attempting to secure safe, affordable and adequate day care. The accompanying press coverage kept the issue on the front burner and provided day care agencies with numerous opportunities to comment publicly on the lack of standards and licensing for their services.

Political action and press coverage paid off, for on July 15, the executive directors of the Group of Three were invited to meet with Mr. Wells and other officials representing his ministry to discuss amendments to the Day Nurseries Act, which had received second reading in the legislature the previous day. The amendments included recognition of family day care in the new legislation. The Group of Three was asked to submit their recommendations for new day care services regulations, as soon as possible. At the meeting, the minister invited the executive directors to meet again before the new law was proclaimed. Royal assent was expected some time early in 1972.

In short order, the Group of Three submitted a five-page document to the provincial government outlining what they considered to be the minimum standards for the delivery of family day care. The standards focused on qualifications, training, ongoing supervision of day care mothers, and the need for them to know and help one another. Although ministry staff developed guidelines for Private Home Day Care in 1973, which many agencies voluntarily adopted, it was not until 1978 that the Day Nurseries Act was amended to require agencies to be licensed, and

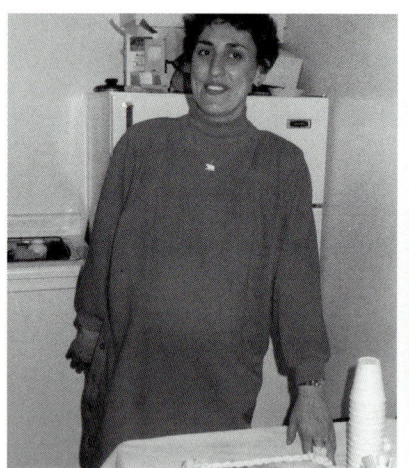

Family Day Care Services

not until 1984 that a fully developed set of standards was implemented.

By March 7, 1972, when a meeting took place between the Group of Three and staff of the Ministry of Social and Family Services, the government still had not amended the Act. At that meeting, the government told the day care agencies that the impending changes would deal exclusively with providing subsidies to those families who qualified as "persons in need," and that the province would assume no responsibility for general standards for family day care. The government took the position that its concern with home day care providers extended only as far as its accountability for spending public money to underwrite a portion of the cost of their services. This was a major disappointment to the Group of Three, who nevertheless urged the government to introduce these funding changes as quickly as possible, believing that the sooner the new legislation was set in place, the sooner its strengths, weaknesses, errors, and omissions would reveal themselves.

By mid-May, the government had still failed to act. Frustrated by the delay, the executive of Family Day Care Services sent the following telegram to Premier William Davis, with copies to the new Minister of Social and Family Services, René Brunelle, and to Allan Lawrence, the local Member of Provincial Parliament:

"Strongly urge immediate release of Regulations governing private home day care. Extended delay causing grave concern, financial stress and curtailment of service."

The telegram precipitated a phone call from an administrative assistant in Mr. Brunelle's office who promised that the regulations permitting cost-sharing of fee subsidies for lower income families would go to Cabinet that week, and that it would be gazetted within two weeks.

At last, in June, the long awaited regulations were enacted. As the following excerpt from the minutes of June 13, 1972 indicates, the regulations were greeted with resignation by Family Day Care Services. The minutes also record the Board's surprise and deep concern over the government's decision to designate a much later date for the bill to take effect than was expected.

"The content of the Regulations is much as expected and

appears to provide a sound and workable basis for initiating family day care programs anywhere throughout the Province. The disappointing factor is the operative date, which has been designated as May 11, rather than the anticipated April 1, or the hoped for January 1.

"This means that 4 1/2 months of service to families who qualify as 'persons in need' will not be eligible for subsidy. This amounts to approximately $60,000 of the $160,000 anticipated from Metro in 1972. Because our service was maintained at 1971 levels (neither expanded nor cut back) and subject to the Province's unexpected decision re: the effective date, we find ourselves in a serious deficit position for 1972. It was recognized that these particular circumstances, which were outside our budgetary and service management control, provides grounds for an approach to Metro and to the Province requesting their assistance in meeting the cost incurred in providing service from January 1 to May 11, 1972."

Letters were sent to Premier Davis and Mr. Brunelle requesting provincial assistance in meeting the 1972 deficit that was incurred as a result of government delay in enacting the regulations, and its decision not to make them retroactive to the first of the year. In October, the Agency received a reply from a Community and Social Services Ministry official expressing the government's regret that it could not provide additional funds, "...since our legislation does not permit authorization of retroactive payments for service provided before the date on which the legislation came into effect."

Throughout the protracted struggle to positively influence the regulatory requirements that would introduce subsidy funding for family day care, the Board of Family Day Care Services was also busy on another front. In June 1971, Miss Quiggin had been approached to help develop a day care centre in Flemingdon Park, a high density, subsidized housing project in North York. By the following year, the Agency had helped to establish a group care program for school-aged children, in a room in the Flemingdon Park Community Centre. The children were cared for from 7:00 a.m. until school began, at noon, when they would receive a nutritious lunch, and again between 3:00 and 6:00 p.m., when they

Family Day Care Services

would again be in the care of their parents.

Also in the early 1970s, the Group of Three wrestled with the question of whether or not to amalgamate. Each agency assigned a number of staff members to sit on a joint committee to examine the pros and cons of such a merger. Between 1971 and 1973, they conducted a lengthy series of meetings, which ultimately led to a decision, in May 1973, to forego any further discussion of combining the three agencies into a single large one. Though they did not join forces under a single banner, the process deepened their reliance upon one another and served to strengthen their collective voice when speaking to government.

The members of the Group of Three were not the only child care advocates who had difficulty being heard by various levels of government in that period. In Metro Toronto, in the early 1970s, mounting frustration over the piecemeal way in which the municipality funded day care centres compelled the operators of a number of them, and a group of single mothers, to band together and take their case to Metro Council. The group included Irene Kyle, a children's program director at Central Neighbourhood House.

"At the time," says Kyle, "there was a lot of work being done at the community level to build day care. Funding was the big issue: how did you go about getting the necessary dollars? There were no ground rules, no workable system. So, we decided to get together to press for proper budget guidelines."

Maria de Wit, who founded and directed the York University Co-operative Day Care Centre, was also a member of that delegation to Metro Toronto.

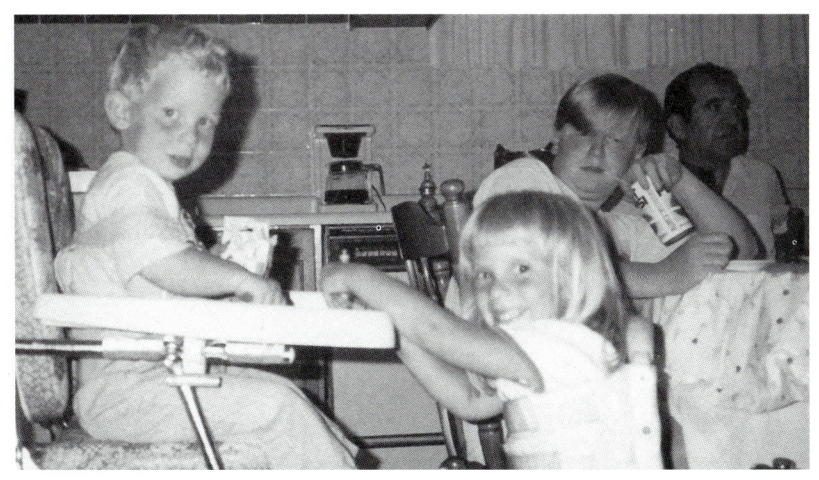

Recalling those days, de Wit says, "It took us years to find out that there was a Social Services Committee (of Metro Council) that actually made the decisions about child care. Nobody seemed to know how anything worked. At the beginning of every month, a man would come and check our roll book for the previous four weeks – huge, red journals, the kind they used in the eighteen hundreds. And he paid us for the previous month's attendance. He'd pay our invoice right then and there. But every 'A' in the roll book would cost us money – 'A' meaning absent. And each one cost us ten dollars. This went on for a long time until we eventually found out about Metro's Social Services Committee. So, Irene Kyle from Central Neighbourhood House, Julie Mathien from the Toronto Board of Education, and I, and a number of community members, tried to make a presentation to this committee but we couldn't get on the agenda. There had to be a child care issue already on the agenda, otherwise you couldn't stand up and speak. And you couldn't simply ask them to put such an item on. You just had to wait until one came up.

"We attended the committee's meetings six or seven times and still weren't permitted to speak. It was getting extremely frustrating and so, for the first time in my career, I agreed that we should bring our kids to a public meeting. Each time we brought the kids, they got noisier and noisier until, at last, Metro Chairman Paul Godfrey said, 'Maybe we'd better hear these people.'

"We stood up and tossed those big leather-bound roll books across the table and I said, 'It doesn't make sense to do things this way. The system isn't working. We think we have ways to improve it based on enrollment, not attendance.' We were told to meet with Metro staff to work out a different system. That turned out to be another long process, but eventually we succeeded.

"Our presentation to the Social Services Committee led it to create a standing sub-committee on child care issues. Thus, Metro's first Child Care Advisory Committee was established, and we sat on that. It was the first such committee anywhere, a forerunner. Before that, child care had had no local voice. No one knew where the funding for child care came from, or that it was a combination of federal, provincial and municipal dollars."

Out of that advisory committee came the impetus for Metro staff to develop the policies and procedures to set up the budgetary process that the community organizers of day care had been asking for.

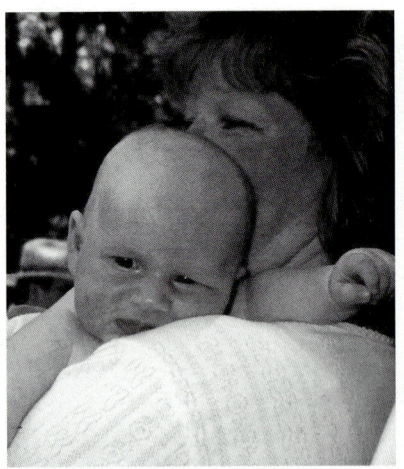

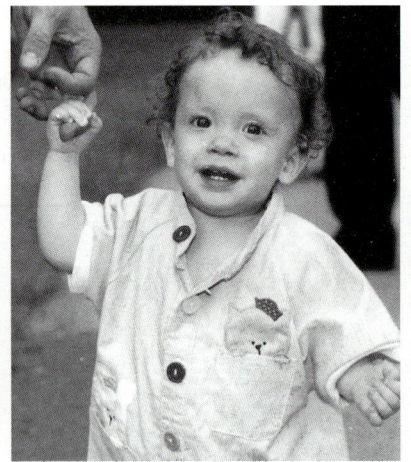

Decades of Change

As the following pages will show, the years between 1971 and 2001 were decades of profound and rapid change for Family Day Care Services. The Agency's leadership, specifically, the composition and philosophy of its Board of Directors, would, over time, undergo a fundamental change, as would the management practices and program priorities of successive Executive Directors. Of course, changes in leadership and management had a direct impact on staff, whose numbers and range of professional skills increased to keep up with more and varied child care programs that the Agency would offer. Since 1971, the number of children cared for has risen from a few dozen to over 4,800, and revenues have increased nearly 100-fold, from $250,000 to almost $25 million in the year 2,000.

Betty Quiggin retired from Family Day Care Services in 1976 and was replaced by Rev. Howard Watson, who stayed with the Agency for approximately a year and a half. In 1978, John Pepin, who proved to be both innovative and entrepreneurial, took over as Executive Director and launched the Agency into a decade that is remembered by longtime staff members as one of the most exciting in the organization's long history.

Program Director Liz Colley, who joined Family Day Care Services in 1982, remembers Pepin's penchant for pushing the limits of the Agency's mandate, in the sense that he was always looking for new approaches to child care.

"He was always trying new ideas and new ways of providing service to families," recalls Colley.

Pepin was the first executive director to actively pursue private corporate sponsorship for some of the programs the Agency undertook during his tenure. In 1982, he was one of the key people behind the founding of the Private Home Day Care Association of Ontario (later, the Home Child Care Association of Ontario), which sought to address the specific concerns of licensed home day care.

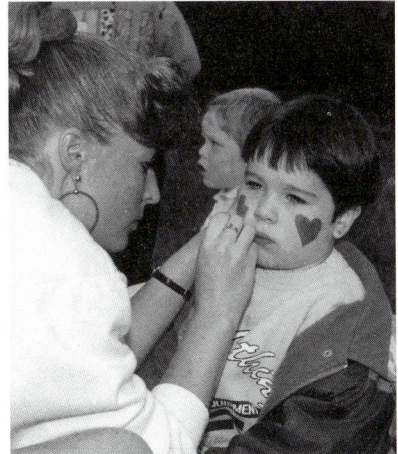

"There's no doubt about it," says Administration and Finance Director Janet Tipton, who came to work at Family Day Care Services in 1980, "John Pepin was an entrepreneurial man. Prior to his arrival, we'd been a very conservative agency. He brought in many innovative changes, which meant that some of the staff moved on to make room for a new team of people who were ready to take the organization in new directions. And for the most part, the Board approved of his initiatives. It was hard for some staff to make the transition from a conventional social service agency to a more commercial service that was bottom line-driven. John was sometimes hard to read, and he had a way of tossing everything upside down and making us look at them in different ways, which was a very different approach for an organization like ours."

Pepin himself recalls that the transition was not always easy. Betty Quiggin and her Board, composed chiefly of men and women from Rosedale and Canada's financial centre, Bay Street, ran the Agency in much the same way that their predecessors, the Lady Managers, had run the Protestant Orphans Home and Female Aid Society, more than a century and a quarter before. They were extremely dedicated people who were committed to serving the needs of children. However, recalls Pepin, the Board tended to be conservative in its outlook and carefully measured every step. Pepin, on the other hand, was a risk-taker. The two in combination worked to strengthen the Agency.

"The Junior League played a major role on the Board of Family Day Care Services," says Pepin. "It's composed chiefly of younger women who engage in charitable volunteer work within their communities. We always had at least one placement on our Board from the Junior League."

Under Pepin, the Board remained influential, acting as strong advocates for children and their families. In later years, a change began in the composition of the Board of Directors that would continue well after Maria de Wit had assumed the executive directorship of the organization in 1988. During that period of transition, the Board gradually came to include people representing a broader spectrum of society.

During the Pepin years, the Agency began to project a higher public profile by sponsoring child care workshops and publishing

Family Day Care Services

articles on the subject and making them available to interested parties, not just in Toronto, but across Canada. As well, John Pepin was able to secure funding from the Levi Strauss Corporation to sponsor child care management workshops across the country.

In the 1980s, the property-casualty insurance industry suffered a case of nerves, thanks to a number of multi-million dollar court awards that had been made to injured persons. Virtually overnight, the industry refused to insure a surprisingly long list of clients, including child care centres, claiming they were a bad risk. As a result, many service providers turned to the Private Home Day Care Association of Ontario and Family Day Care Services to act as their advocate on the issue.

"I was on Peter Gzowski (CBC's national morning radio show, *Morningside*) a number of times. We just lobbied like crazy, did a lot of PR work, and forced the insurance industry to insure child care centres. So, we used our clout and our size to have a major influence on child care issues."

Pepin also changed the way in which the Agency was funded. He set up a number of revenue centres. One such revenue centre, and the only one completely funded by the provincial government, was the Private Home Day Care for Developmentally Handicapped Children (known after 1991 as the Home Child Care Program for Children with Developmental Delays). Pepin is especially proud of this groundbreaking initiative, because, to get it up and running, he had to overcome resistance from certain naysayers who claimed regular home day care was not an option for developmentally challenged children.

"This was the first such program anywhere. It was a major coup. Children with and without developmental challenges were integrated into the homes. We provided special training, equipment and support."

Since Family Day Care Services was the first agency to provide such a service, the regulatory structure to deliver such a program had not yet been set in place.

"All the funding and all the government policies, the entire legislative framework flowed from that experience," says Pepin. "But it took us about two or three years of lobbying to convince people we could do it, and that the children didn't have to be in institutional settings. I'd say that was one of the most important contributions we made in that period.

"Originally, some people in the field were not positive about it because they didn't think that we could care for the children in private homes; we couldn't have paraprofessionals doing a good job. So, we had to convince them – first by agreeing to work only with 'easier' kids. But almost immediately, we were inundated by applications to care for children with multiple challenges and we demonstrated that we could work with them.

"That was really great! And it was a significant part of the whole normalization process that was taking place during that era. I think that was a big contribution, from a program standpoint, that the organization made."

Under John Pepin, the Agency also devised and operated some decidedly commercial ventures, which were a radical departure from the standard not-for-profit services it had come to be known for. As an example, in 1979, the Agency introduced Day Care Finders, a full-fee home day care program for Metro Toronto parents who could afford to pay the entire cost of their children's care. Over the next four years, this program expanded into Mississauga, Brampton, and the Region of York. In 1986, after five children and a private day care provider (not associated with the Agency) died in a house fire in Bolton, the Ministry of Community and Social Services freed up funding for family day care to allow the Day Care Finders program to expand into that community. The following year, the program was expanded to include fee-assisted families from York Region. And in 1988, Day Care Finders began serving the employees of Toronto's Hospital for Sick Children. The program would change and expand even further under Maria de Wit.

In the early years of the Pepin era, in 1980, the Agency began offering day care consulting services to large, private corporations. Another enterprise, which was sold to employers for their employees, was an employee assistance program that specialized in child care information, referral, and counselling. Called the Working Parents Day Care Assurance Program, it was inaugurated by Pepin in 1982.

"We created this program and then we franchised it. And it

was the first time a charity had ever franchised anything. We sold the idea to a commercial (day care) vendor in Ottawa and to a charity in British Columbia," says Pepin.

The program expanded into Montreal. In 1991, under Maria de Wit, it was streamlined with yet another of the profit-making initiatives taken by the Agency in the 1980s, the Elder Care Program, later known as the Elder Life Plan. Acting upon a management study that concluded there was a need for elder care in Toronto, the Agency offered seniors private home day care in their own residences. The Working Parents Day Care Assurance Program and the Elder Life Plan were combined in 1991 to form part of the Agency's Corporate Support Services. Their client list contained the names of 17 major companies, including the Xerox Corporation. Agency staff met face-to-face with the employees of their corporate clients to advise them of their day care options. It was a trustworthy nationwide service that linked employees with approved day care providers across Canada. However, it could not compete on price with lower cost automated services that required only a phone operator and a computer-driven database. In 1995, the Agency was obliged to withdraw the service.

These programs did much to enhance the quality of employee assistance programs (EAPs) across Canada. Previously, EAPs had confined themselves to the health and well being of the individual employee. By focusing attention on child and elder day care, the Agency raised awareness in Corporate Canada that healthy families were as fundamentally important to their employees as their employees' health. Organizations learned that if they provided employees with programs designed to meet their family needs, their employees grew more at ease and were better able to function productively at work.

In the mid-1980s, the Agency also established the Temporary Child care Program, yet another form of respite care. This program was offered on an emergency basis to working parents whose children were ill and unable to go to their regular home child care giver. In such cases, the Agency sent a caregiver to the child's home until the child was well enough to resume a normal day care routine. This program was eventually cancelled by the Agency in 1989 for lack of adequate funding.

The needs of young mothers were also of great concern to Agency staff. In 1981, Family Day Care Services joined community advocates, such as writer June Callwood, the Ministry of Community and Social Services, Metro Toronto's Public Health Department, the Children's Aid Society, and individuals living in downtown Toronto, to establish Jessie's Centre for Teenagers, a support service for adolescent parents and their infants. Young mothers were encouraged to drop into the centre, where they would receive professional counselling and the support of their peers. A Family Day Care Services worker was seconded to Jessie's to deliver a 24-hour-a-day emergency respite care program for teen moms who experienced difficulties coping with their roles as parents. Once the program was established and operating successfully, Jessie's assumed full responsibility for its own operation. Today, Jessie's continues to offer much needed assistance to approximately 500 families.

There was even a brief attempt to launch a nanny service, but it was soon abandoned because the Agency could not ensure that the service would be financially viable, or that its reputation for high standards would be maintained.

The Home Day Care Program, which began in East York, is one program that has grown significantly over the years in response to growing demand. It exists today as one of the two core programs provided by Family Day Care Services to families living in the Regions of Peel and York and certain districts of the City of Toronto. In 1980, the program expanded into Etobicoke, when the Agency took over that municipality's Home Day Care Program, which had been run by a non-profit agency that had intended to terminate it. In 1986, the program expanded into Scarborough. For the next seven years, the number of families served by it in East York, North York, Etobicoke, and Scarborough remained stable. It was not until 1993 that the Home Day Care Program got its biggest boost, which came in the form of the Agency's biggest challenge. Before that happened, though, John Pepin would leave the Agency and Maria de Wit would join Family Day Care Services.

After leaving York University's Co-operative Day Care Centre, which she ran between 1972 and 1979, de Wit worked for ten years as the Assistant Director of the Metro Toronto Children's Services

Division, where she developed policy and program activities in the field of child care. She had a background in finance and business administration and was a popular lecturer in the Early Childhood Development Program at George Brown College. Over the years, she had also been seconded several times to the Ministry of Community and Social Services. Clearly, Maria de Wit was eminently qualified for the job of Executive Director of Family Day Care Services. But she was also extremely well connected politically and knew that the provincial government was considering changes in the way home day care was operated. She was faced with the decision of staying in a secure job with Metro that she thoroughly enjoyed, or taking on a new position with an organization whose future might be very much in doubt. Nevertheless, when she was asked in what direction she would take the Agency, if she decided to accept the job, she answered, "I'd expand its services and integrate the home-based child care programs the Agency already runs with centre-based care."

Prior to Maria de Wit's preliminary discussions with Family Day Care Services, the provincial government had announced that every new primary school built in Ontario had to include a child day care centre.

"There you are!" said de Wit to the members of the search team. "There's your capital. You go for every school in the communities where you already provide home day care, and you give the parents a choice."

De Wit's recommendation was passed onto the Board. It was made clear that if they decided to hire her, they would have to make a commitment to expand into centre-based child care. On May 1, 1988, Maria de Wit became the new Executive Director of Family Day Care Services.

Shortly after the Agency submitted and received approval of proposals to the Peel and York Boards of Education to establish Family Day Care Centres in some of their soon-to-be-built elementary schools.

Recalling the Agency's entry into centre-based care, Liz Colley said, "Family Day Care Services was in the right place at the right time. With all the new schools that were opening up in the regional municipalities of Peel and York, once we'd been approved for one or two, it was natural that we should have been contracted for more. Best of all, we didn't have to pay for the buildings. The Ministries of Education and Community and Social Services were in partnership. The school boards provided the space, the provincial government paid for supplies and equipment, and Family Day Care Services hired the staff to operate the program in each centre."

There followed a series of school-based child care centre openings in Toronto, Mississauga, Brampton, Markham, Richmond Hill, Thornhill, and Newmarket. As part of this period of rapid expansion, in 1993, the Agency was given the responsibility of managing the Ministry of Community and Social Services' conversion initiative whereby commercial child care centres were converted to non-profit operations. In 1994, a partnership agreement with the Dufferin-Peel Separate School Board led to the opening of the St. Francis Xavier Child Care Centre for infant children to age six, in Mississauga. Since the first school-based centres opened in 1989, the Agency's network of centres in Toronto and the Regions of Peel and York has expanded to 25. Collectively, they care for approximately 2,400 children, or approximately half of all the children served by the Agency, the other 2,400 being cared for in private homes affiliated with Family Day Care Services.

Of particular interest is the child care centre that was established in Hagerman House, a pioneer farmhouse built around 1855, now designated as a heritage building, at the corner of 14th Avenue and Birchmount Road in Markham. After acquiring the property in 1994, an ambitious capital campaign was launched to underwrite the cost of restorations and renovations. The centre opened a year later to serve children from six weeks to six years of age. Incorporated within the centre are the administrative offices for the Agency's centre-based and home care operations in the Regional Municipality of York.

According to former Board chair, Dr. John Fauquier, the acquisition and transformation of Hagerman House illustrated very well Maria de Wit's considerable capabilities as a manager.

Fauquier and the rest of the Board had already seen ample evidence of their Executive Director's ability to seize an opportunity for the Agency and, with the help of senior staff, finesse it to a successful conclusion. The year before, on July 12, 1993, the Regional Municipality of Peel's Social Services Commissioner, Paul Vezina, had announced that in the fall the municipality would no longer provide home day care to approximately 1,000 children in Peel. This decision was taken because of the fear that discussions about provider unionization in Toronto and Ottawa would spread to other areas of Ontario, and if providers were granted employee status, it could lead to significant cost increases that would not be matched by government funding.

Cheryl Rogers, who used to work as a supervisor in the Region's home child care program, and who now manages the program for Family Day Care Services, was as surprised as the rest of her colleagues at Vezina's announcement.

"It came right out of the blue," she recalls. "We were just called in and told that as of September 4, the program was closing. No one had any idea what would happen to the children or to the caregivers. The Region had approached COMSOC (the Ministry of Community and Social Services) in search of someone else to operate the program. The parents, the caregivers, the children, Peel employees like me – all of us were in limbo. Letters were sent to all the parents."

Caregivers from across the Region banded together to fight the decision, but it was to no avail. Council had made up its mind. As staff members, Cheryl Rogers and her co-workers had always been discouraged from attending council meetings. But after the announcement was made and the issue heated up, they were asked to be present. Caregivers, parents, and children packed the public gallery.

Rogers said, "People got up and made presentations, but it was a *fait accompli*. The councillors weren't really listening. They just said, 'Sorry. Social Contract.' (an erroneous reference to a fiscal initiative taken by the NDP government of Premier Bob Rae that had nothing whatever to do with the real reason the Region had withdrawn from home day care). Roads, water, sewers come before day care."

When representatives of the provincial government asked Maria de Wit if Family Day Care Services would be interested in taking over Peel's home day care program, she referred the matter to the Board.

"We had to make a decision," says John Fauquier. "Did we want to take on something that would compel us to almost double the size of the Agency? We decided that we were prepared to do that, but the provincial government would have to come up with the money to pay for our transition costs. Which they did."

The Agency was committed. And with only a matter of weeks before the Region of Peel's program came to an end, leaving hundreds of households with no day care, Maria de Wit and her staff got busy.

"My respect for Maria had been growing steadily," recalls Fauquier, "but she utterly astounded me this time! Our first meeting with the province took place in mid-August. By October 2 – about a month and a half later – our first satellite office, located at the corner of Derry Road and Tomken Road, had been rented, decorated, furnished, equipped, staffed, and was up and running. And in that time, she and her staff had virtually doubled the size of the Agency."

Jean Wise, Program Manager for Peel Home Child Care, remembers the excitement she felt during those frantic six weeks. She divided her time between interviewing prospective employees, parents, and caregivers. There was also an enormous amount of paperwork that had to be dealt with and information transferred from the Region before the transition was complete.

"We had no office, so I had to work out of the trunk of my car," she recalls. "I would go home at the end of the day exhausted and say to my husband, 'I can't do this! It's just too overwhelming!' But then I'd get up next morning and do it all over again."

In the midst of all this expansion, the Agency remained committed to providing quality programming to the children and families it served. The Day Care Finders program became known as the Agency's Home Child Care programs in Peel and York Regions, and in Toronto. In 1993, the High/Scope Curriculum was introduced into all child care centres. The curriculum was first developed in the United States in the early 1970s as part of the work to strengthen Head Start and other early childhood development programs, and had grown out of the work of

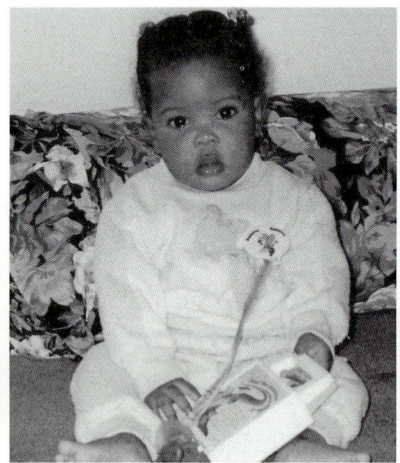

American developmental psychologist, Dr. David Weikart.

According to Program Resource Consultant Jill Poisson, who first introduced High/Scope into Family Day Care Services child care centres, the curriculum is highly enriching for children and a major departure from conventional, teacher-initiated learning, which relies on large group activities with the teacher at the centre. With High/Scope, all activities are performed in small groups with one staff member for every eight children.

"High/Scope provides a much more practical approach, since children learn best when they learn actively," says Poisson. "We discourage a lot of teacher-initiated learning because the children are not at an age when they can physically or intellectually cope with that kind of environment."

The children plan their own day. Everything they do is based on what are referred to in the High/Scope lexicon as "key experiences." For example, before children can learn to read and write, they need to know how to classify things, seriate (put things in their proper order), group things together, and separate things. And before they can learn to tell time, they must first understand what is meant by "before" and "after."

Program Resource Consultant Lisa Pecarski says, "We set up our play room with all of these key experiences in mind. That's how we're able to observe the children develop, and we're then able to share this information with the parents."

Though introduced a few years later in Canada, High/Scope has been around long enough in the U.S. for David Weikart to have charted its impact on the lives of the people who were introduced to the curriculum as children 30 years ago. He has been able to compare their development and performance against that of children who experienced conventional child care curricula or none at all.

Says Pecarski, "Weikart found that nearly 30 years down the road, the children who were exposed to the High/Scope curriculum earned higher than average incomes, stayed in school longer and thus attained higher levels of education, ran afoul of the law less often – though when they did, for some curious reason they tended to commit acts of vandalism more often than their peers did."

Weikart's curriculum also carries within it lessons on how to

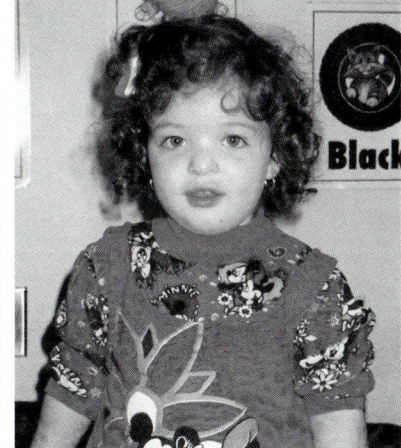

150 Years of Caring for Children and Families

get along with others. Children are exposed to several key experiences that help them to build social relationships with those around them. One of these is conflict resolution. The children learn how to listen and to talk to one another. Infants and toddlers learn to take turns, to share toys and equipment and to build relationships with their teachers and the other children in the room. Incorporated within the program is an anti-bullying component and lessons that teach children how to resolve conflicts with one another without the need for their teacher to intervene.

By the time the children reach school age, they have become experienced problem solvers, say Pecarski. "We are now going to work with our children in all Family Day Care Services child care centres to compile our own studies that we hope will tell us if conflict resolution techniques have a long-lasting effect."

Because Canada lags behind the United States, where many jurisdictions have adopted the High/Scope curriculum from kindergarten to grade eight, the program does not mesh well with the Canadian kindergarten program, which relies, of necessity, on large group, teacher-led experiences. "Nevertheless," says Lisa Pecarski, "High/Scope provides children with a good start."

Home caregivers are actively encouraged to incorporate into their work some of High/Scope's core principles. Though contracted, trained, and supervised by Family Day Care Services, home day caregivers are self-employed. They care for children who range in age from infancy to pre-teens, who arrive at, and leave, the day care home at different hours each day, and who, developmentally, are at different stages in their lives. Moreover, home care providers don't have the expensive play and educational equipment that the centres do. Nevertheless, home caregivers provide a higher degree of one-on-one care, which many parents want for their children. The Agency assists home caregivers to set up an environment that is conducive to learning.

Says Lisa Pecarski, "A program's only as good as its environment. So we try to teach the same environmental concepts to home care givers that we use in the centres. That means that in the day care home you have a book area where kids can read or look at pictures quietly. You put your block play area near your pretend play area because the activities that go on there tend to be a bit noisy, but it allows for a lot of creativity and a lot of big movement."

Five times a year, the Agency's 600 home caregivers receive resource kits, large plastic "goodie bags" containing glue, craft and tissue paper, stickers, and pages of suggestions for fun and creative activities in which the children can involve themselves. Since the caregivers and the children represent a rich and diverse ethnic and cultural mix, none of the activities are sectarian or tied to any ethnic group. Instead, they celebrate seasonal changes or activities that all of the women and children can participate in. Thus, instead of celebrating Halloween, which is associated with the Christian tradition, the goodie bags contain activities connected to the colour orange. In December, the theme may be snow pals instead of snowmen and Christmas. The care that Lisa Pecarski and her colleagues take in selecting materials for their resource kits demonstrates their determination to be as inclusive of every cultural and ethnic background and tradition as they possible can. It also speaks to their commitment to Family Day Care Services'

Anti-Racism Policy, which was drafted by the Agency in 1992, and which was the first step taken by any Canadian child care agency to address a growing serious societal problem. In fact, the Agency led the way in fashioning an HIV/AIDS Policy in 1994, and harassment Policy in 1999.

The relationships that exist between the Agency's home and centre-based day care workers and the children who trustingly come to them every day has long been recognized as special, something to be protected and nurtured. Their bond is as strong as those that existed between the orphans and matrons during the Agency's orphanage years, and those that existed between foster mothers and children during the Agency's foster period.

150 Years of Caring for Children and Families

143

Introducing Strangers to Strangers

In Ontario, in 1995, approximately 9% of home child care arrangements were regulated; the rest were informal arrangements worked out between parents and relatives, friends and, in a large number of cases, strangers. Provincial standards under the Day Nurseries Act govern only child care providers who are affiliated with agencies; they must also meet local fire, health, and safety regulations. Child care advocates like Maria de Wit often wonder if every person who provides day care services to non-relatives should be directly licensed and, therefore, accountable for the quality of the care they provide to children.

In respect of accountability she says, "I've always wondered why people need a license to drive a taxi, or run a restaurant, but nobody needs a license to look after children.

"As far as Family Day Care Services is concerned, we hold the licence, so we are accountable for the care our home care providers give. And since these women are with the children every day, and our supervisors are there only so many days a month, the Agency has to strengthen the ability of these women to do a good job. And we've been doing things this way for 35 years. Quality is not determined by standards and licensing alone. It has everything to do with *how* you support, encourage and help to educate caregivers to provide services that will meet our standards."

Since the vast majority of home child care arrangements are unregulated, de Wit is sometimes asked why there is a need for an agency like Family Day Care Services in Greater Toronto.

"In a vast urban area like this, families don't known each other the way they used to years ago. And many of them certainly don't know the people who look after their children every day. So, we introduce strangers to strangers."

Over the years, Family Day Care Services has grown to become Ontario's largest provider of home and centre-based child care services, but according to Maria de Wit, the Agency's

Family Day Care Services

pre-eminence has more to do with the willingness of the members of its management team to involve themselves in the communities they serve than with its $25 million a year operating budget.

"Every member of the management team spends time in the community, helping out with a range of grassroots initiatives that sometimes have to do with our business, but often don't," says de Wit. She herself exemplifies that spirit of involvement by chairing Toronto's Child Care Advisory Committee, and by sitting on a number of other committees, such as the Children and Youth Action Committee.

One of the ways Family Day has continued to demonstrate leadership in home child care during the 1990s has been through its work with other agencies to resolve a number of issues arising from the lack of clarity about providers' employment status in child care and labour legislation. When home child care was first introduced, it was seen as a variation of foster care. The idea was that mothers who were already at home caring for their young children could take in a few extra children to help out their neighbors who worked outside of the home, and, at the same time, earn a few dollars on the side. "Good" care was seen as an extension of "good" mothering.

Over time, however, with increasing agency involvement and a growing professional interest in promoting quality care, agencies began to introduce a number of orientation, training and support programs for providers. In 1978, with the introduction of government regulations for home child care, expectations of providers became more formal, and so providers were subject to inspection not only by agency home visitors, but also by municipal and provincial government officials. Although the demands on providers increased, they continued to be paid as though they were independent workers, and so were not eligible for minimum wage or basic benefits such as vacation and maternity leave, or unemployment insurance. The combination of long hours of work, increased professional expectations, together with government-set provider rates that were often lower than the going community rates, led to discontent among some day care providers. In 1995, in the hope of addressing some of these problems, providers from Macaulay Child Development Centre and Andrew Fleck Child

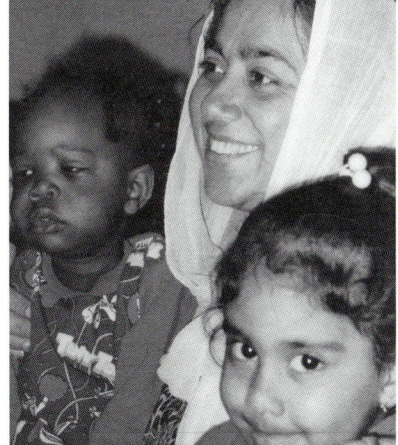

Care Centre in Ottawa initiated a unionization process.

This process raised a number of questions about providers' employment status. Although home child care agencies and child care legislation had always assumed that providers were independent workers, when challenged, their status under labour legislation was unclear and inconsistent – in some assessments they were judged to be employees, in others, as dependent contractors or independent workers. This lack of clarity about provider status, together with fears about the increased costs associated with employee status and the potential changes in the way of work associated with it, led a number of home child care agencies to initiate a review of the way home child care was operated. In 1994, under the umbrella of the Home Child Care Association of Ontario, a number of agencies participated in discussions to develop three alternative models of home child care that would clarify providers' employment status, preserve quality, and still be economically viable. While officials from the Ministry of Community and Social Services sat in on the discussions and initially expressed a willingness to fund the development of pilot projects to test out these new approaches, government funding to support these efforts was cut when the Conservative government came to power. As a consequence, the issues related to providers' status and the development of an alternative model of home child care were never tested or resolved.

In 1996, the question of provider employment status resurfaced again, when a home child care provider from Wellington County filed a complaint with the Ontario Pay Equity Commission claiming employee status and expressing her concern that providers had been left out of the region's pay equity plan. While the Commission's hearings were lengthy and took a number of years, the Tribunal's decision was that the provider was an employee and therefore eligible for pay equity payments. This decision was appealed by the County and was still under litigation at the end of 2000.

In the meantime, however, many agencies were becoming increasingly concerned about the potential financial impact on their services if other providers followed suit. Agencies were caught in the middle – they were expected to comply with pay equity requirements on one hand – while on the other, child care funding did not recognize these additional costs. In the absence of government support, the Board of Family Day Care Services took the initiative and sponsored a "think tank" bringing together many of the larger home child care agencies in the province. The group, which met at the Elora Mill in May 1999, shared information about the current dilemmas facing home child care and reaffirmed the need to re-think the way home child care was delivered and to test out other approaches to service. Following these meetings, a working group of agencies, "the Elora Group" – Family Day Care Services, Andrew Fleck Child Care Services, Macaulay Child Development Centre, Network Child Care Services, Today's Family – Caring for you Child, and the Home Child Care Program of the Regional Municipality of Waterloo, began follow-up meetings to consider what might be involved in an alternative framework for the provision of home child care.

After much background research, group members remained convinced of the need for change – not only to resolve questions about providers' employment status, but also, of the need to improve the quality of care and extend it to more children and families. Further, they thought that it was important to adapt the service to the newer, more holistic thinking that sees home child care as a family support service, and part of an integrated network of community services.

As part of the background research, the Board of Family Day Care Services commissioned Irene Kyle to carry out a critical review of the theoretical and research literature on quality in home child care settings. This monograph was subsequently supported by the City of Toronto and the Regional Municipality of Ottawa-Carleton, as well as by other members of the Elora Group. The long-term goal of the group is to develop an alternative model of home child care and to carry out a demonstration project to evaluate its feasibility and effectiveness. While the details of the model are still being worked out by group members, the goal of their work is to develop an alternative framework that maintains and enhances the quality of home child care for all children by requiring all providers (caring for unrelated children) to be licensed; extends education, resource and support programs to all

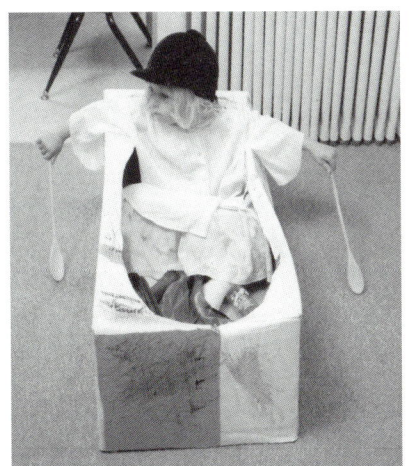

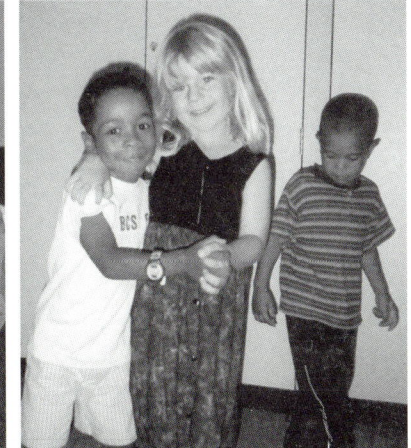

150 Years of Caring for Children and Families

community caregivers; raises the value of carework and the status of providers; enhances the partnership between providers and agency staff; and develops supportive linkages with other child and family services in the community.

A Change of Leadership and Name

Since the mid-1990s, as a result of a recruitment drive that enticed an ethnically richer and more gender-balanced group of people to join the Board, the leadership of Family Day Care Services has also been more involved in the community than it had ever been before.

"We put an ad in the *Toronto Star* and got 150 applications. Here we were advertising for board members who wouldn't receive a dime for their time, and in fact might even find themselves being 'hit up' for money sometimes. We ranked the applications, which included a biography of each person, and conducted interviews. We ended up with a more egalitarian Board whose members really do represent the ethnic make-up of the community – with all the respect that is due the members of previous boards, but who tended to occupy only the top rungs of the economic and social ladder," says Board member John Fauquier.

Another Board member, Bob Hollingshead, worked with Fauquier and de Wit on the selection team.

"I remember how impressed the three of us were by the qualifications of these people," recalls Hollingshead. "Many of them were highly qualified in the field of child care. As a result, the contribution that the Board has been able to make has been tremendous."

The quest for new blood on the Board also attracted a number of professionals representing other disciplines.

"Of course we have lawyers and accountants," says current Board president, Liz Howson. "You need people who understand the law and numbers. But we also have social service workers, a psychologist, management consultants, parents who are clients, a labour specialist, and any number of people who understand public policy issues."

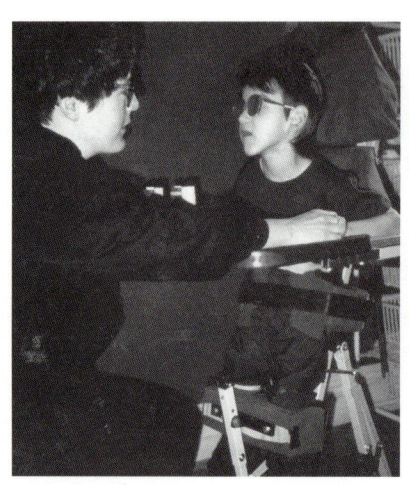

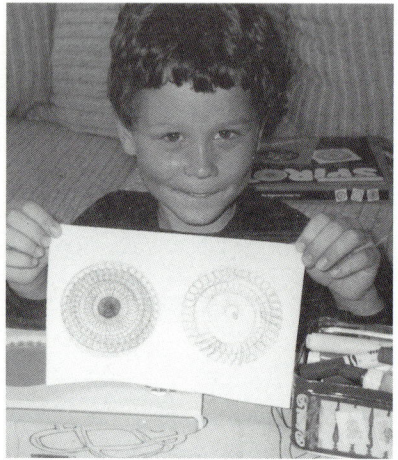

Not long after the Board reconstituted itself, it tackled the issue of governance – the way in which the Agency would be run and the direction it would take. The guide for this important board renewal exercise, called *Carverization*, would be the work of U.S. management consultant John Carver, who asserted that all boards of directors, especially those that run non-profit organizations, should concern themselves exclusively with means, and that staff should concern themselves only with ends. In other words, the Board should deal with global issues, the organization's policies, its budgets, and the overall direction to be taken, while staff members put into action Board decisions. The result was a Board that was much more involved and better informed.

Says John Fauquier, "When I joined the Board in the 1980s, we were assigned to sit on various committees – personnel committee, program committee, finance committee, those sorts of things. They tended to meet around noon. Often, the meetings were rushed and we found that the staff had already done their work. All we seemed to do was rubber stamp their reports. There was poor information flow and very little governance. We did a Board renewal exercise in the mid-90s and imposed the principles of John Carver. I think we were quite successful because today, there are no longer any standing committees, just the odd ad hoc committee, say, to deal with short-term projects like selling our building. Instead, we have general committee, or committee of the whole, and board meetings are fun. We get things done. When we table government policy issues, or advocacy issues, things get pretty passionate!"

Maria de Wit agrees that the Carverization of the Board has yielded wonderful dividends.

"But," she says, "sometimes, when we have a meeting, I can't get them to leave!"

Changing the way in which the Agency markets and promotes itself was among the dividends that accrued from scrutinizing and improving Agency governance. In 1995, with the assistance of a newly appointed marketing consulting firm, the Agency developed a new name, a new logo, and a new slogan. "Family Day" became the Agency's brand name, under a simple but powerfully expressive line drawing of a child being held in the protective arms of an adult, above the slogan "Next to You, We Care the Most."

Says Maria de Wit, "With these changes, we found a way to express what we had known all along: that parents are first and foremost in the lives of children, and we, as an Agency, are the helpers. We support families, and we can never care as much as their families."

Two years later, the Agency also conducted in-house customer service training to deepen staff and board members' understanding of what it really means to serve children and their families. The central thrust of customer service training was reinforced by in-house family-centred training, which the Agency conducted at the same time.

"When we looked at both of these training initiatives, we suddenly experienced a blinding flash of the obvious," recalls Maria de Wit. "They were one and the same. And we realized that, to be successful, every staff and board member had to internalize the principles of customer and family-centred training."

Since Family Day employs approximately 300 people, that internalization process did not happen overnight. However, by the time every staff member had been through the training, a period of a year and a half, it did happen. People talked about it informally over coffee and in staff meetings until, eventually, everyone had both heard and absorbed the message.

Today, all of Family Day's policies and practices are based on family-centred child care, which sees families from an ecological perspective, meaning staff considers the child in the context of the total family and the larger community. There is recognition of the interrelationships and interconnectedness between the child, his or her family and community, and society at large. Families have strengths, they're unique and multidimensional. Most importantly, families are the primary influence on the lives of their children.

Mississauga December 1995

Jordan Richards is a very happy and excited two-year-old. This is his first day at the Hazel McCallion Child Care Centre. He can hardly wait to get through the door. Throughout the past week, Jordy's mother, Kim, and Syl, his father, have been preparing their son for the moment he would wave goodbye, strike out on his own, and meet new friends. Since Kim is obliged to be at her office this morning, Syl must take Jordy to the Centre. He unzips the toddler's winter coat and tugs off his toque to reveal a mass of black curls and a pair of cheeks that neither of his grandparents have been able to resist pinching since he was born.

Jordy's teacher, Beth, greets father and son at the front door. With no hesitation, Jordy walks confidently into the brightly-lit and colourfully decorated room and begins to play with the other children. Summarily dismissed, though grateful that his son hadn't dissolved into tears, Syl has a quick word with Beth and leaves.

Later that day, when Syl arrives to pick Jordy up, Beth hands him a card in the shape of a snowman. On the card, she wrote:

"Kim and Syl:

"Jordy had a great first day! He said goodbye to Dad with no tears and participated in all the activities. He had a few tears during transition times, but settled down quickly once we were involved. He ate half a serving of lunch and settled down on his bed nicely (no crying, fell asleep about one o'clock). We sang a lot of songs and had a lot of cuddles. He's a great addition to our room! If you have any questions or concerns, feel free to see me. – Beth.

"p.s. The ABC song brought quite a reaction."

When Beth sang the ABC song to Jordy, as she was changing his diaper, the little fellow burst into tears and sobbed, "My mommy sings me that song."

In the course of the next year, Jordy settled comfortably into what his parents came to regard as his "second home." Their relationship with Beth deepened until she was thought of as a member of the family. But everything comes to an end, and Beth's association with Family Day was no exception. She had decided to further her education. She would leave the Agency early in the New Year.

150 Years of Caring for Children and Families

Mississauga January 1997
"Kim and Syl:
"It's hard to believe the time has come to say goodbye. I don't have to tell you how much I've enjoyed working with Jordy and getting to know you both. Jordy is an incredible little boy with a lot of spunk and drive. His charm has made my stay here a memorable one. He is a happy little boy who's sensitive and bright. You've done a wonderful job with him. He's even inspired me to have kids (in the future, that is). I will miss him terribly and think of him often. – Beth.
"p.s. My mornings won't be the same without those hugs!"

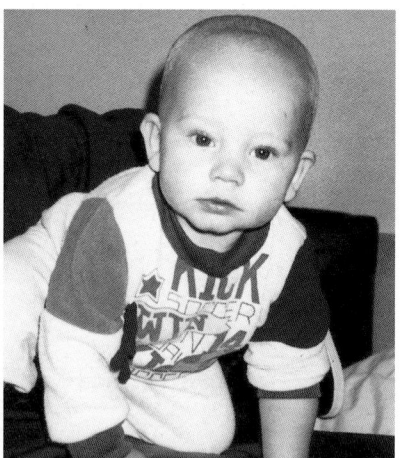

Jordy

Family Day Care Services

The Fourth Paradigm

What lies ahead for Family Day? After 150 years of meeting the needs of children and their families, what services, or package of services, as Bob Hollingshead refers to them, will the Agency offer to families?

"Quality day care is and always will be of fundamental importance, especially in the early years of a child's development," he insists. "For us to survive and to thrive, we're going to have to be very open-minded about new ideas. Of course, what happens to Family Day is important to a large number of people. The Agency is considered a leader in promoting quality child care. And we've always been committed to finding solutions to families' needs. That's where our strength lies."

One way in which Family Day might provide solutions for families, says Maria de Wit, is in the area of caregiver training and education.

"I see us extending our education programs to include parents," she says. "If we had some community resource programs, they could be available to everyone who cares for children, whether they be parents or caregivers. But we'd have to find a way to do that efficiently. The trouble is space. It's expensive. And the government funding for family support services is still very limited. Perhaps there's a solution somewhere. We'll have to explore it.

"We're going through a paradigm shift, and it's towards the support of families. It's not only by providing child care that we can support families. The Agency should be in any business that helps families raise good citizens," says de Wit.

John Fauquier agrees. He and his colleagues on the Board are in favour of any initiative that will raise the bar higher.

"It's about quality care. We're constantly asking ourselves, 'Where we can take child care from here? What more can we do?' We constantly push ourselves into research, push ourselves into policy issues."

With Fauquier as its driving force, the Board of Family Day has, for the past few years, pursued the development of Canada's

150 Years of Caring for Children and Families

first Centre for Child Care Excellence. When he first proposed the idea, his fellow Board members wanted to know what this "institute" would be like. He told them that at first there'd be no bricks and mortar, not even an office. Instead, Family Day would sponsor working luncheons and seminars. Perhaps, he said, they'd fund child care research. They would celebrate excellence within the Agency among staff members, and they'd strengthen connections with the academic community and their sister agencies in the field. And because Family Day is a major presence in that field, the Agency was in a great position to make things happen. Eventually the Board endorsed the concept of a Centre for Excellence.

The first initiative the Centre took was to sponsor research being conducted into home child care by Irene Kyle, who then was a doctoral student at the University of Guelph. Kyle's interest in doing the study grew out of a concern that much of the existing research in home child care had not consulted with providers directly about their knowledge and experience and had often ignored their needs as care workers. Rather than taking providers and their work for granted, the study took provider's experiences as the starting point and sought to learn more about how providers made sense of their work of caring for other people's children. Kyle interviewed 15 agency-affiliated and 15 independent home child care providers in Toronto and several smaller communities in southwest Ontario. Providers' accounts of their experiences of caring for children were very insightful and helped Kyle to understand the supports and working conditions providers require if they are to nurture children and support their families on an ongoing basis. Kyle is clear about the important role the Centre played in helping to support her research: "In Canada, it is difficult to find funding to support any research in child care. Without financial and on-going moral support from Maria de Wit and the Board, I wouldn't have been able to carry out this study."

Providers' comments about what made for "good" care led to an interest in how quality is defined in home child care, and eventually to Kyle's preparation of the background report on quality for the Centre.

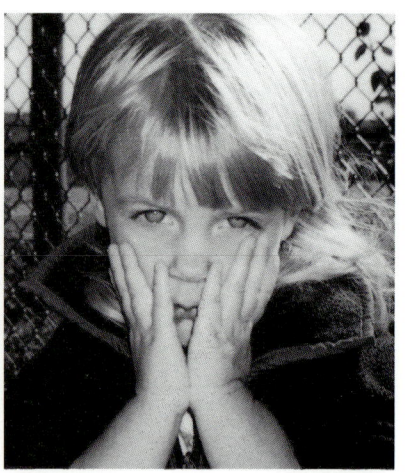

Says Fauquier, "The thing that really got the Centre off the ground, though, was our association with Professors Bruce Ryan and Donna Lero of the Department of Family Studies (now the Department of Family Relations and Applied Nutrition) of the University of Guelph."

It was agreed that in May 1998, Family Day and the University would sponsor a conference at the Metro Convention Centre at which faculty members and graduate students would present papers on child care. The papers dealt with applied research because both the Agency and the University sought to extract practical ideas for use by the entire field of child care.

"Our working relationship with the folks at the University was divine from day one," recalls Fauquier, "Family Day looked after the logistics – provided the facility, did the promotion, helped get the papers published in the Canadian Journal of Research in Early Childhood Education. For their part, the University put out notices for papers, reviewed the abstracts that were submitted by the students – the academic piece of the puzzle. We stuck to our respective roles and recognized the mutual benefits that would accrue to the University and the Agency. Our keynote speaker was children's author, Robert Munsch, who had been an adjunct professor in that same faculty at the University. We all felt the day was a great success because that kind of thing had never been done before."

The notion of a Centre for Child Care Excellence blends well with Maria de Wit's desire to extend child care training to anyone who might be interested, and could one day lead to Family Day making a wide range of helpful child-based information available on its web site.

"There are no limitations on new ways of communicating, new ways of providing services," says Fauquier. "But more than anything, will the Centre for Child Care *Excellence* – and that's the key word – raise the bar in child care? Will it provoke people to serve children and their families better – more efficiently and in a caring way? If it does, we will have succeeded."

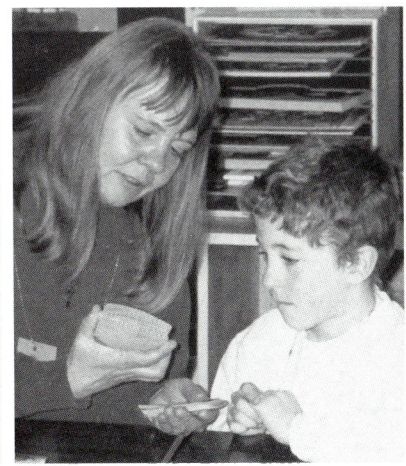

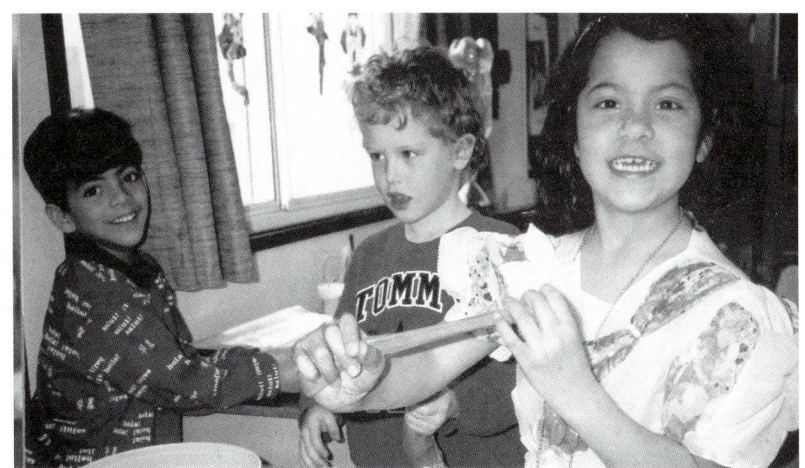

Postscript

In 1851, illness or death of one or both parents was the primary reason a child came into the care of the Protestant Orphans' Home and Female Aid Society. In those days, the Lady Managers believed it was their mission to rescue the city's underprivileged and homeless children. Since the task they set for themselves was born both of religious conviction and recognition of their duty as members of the ruling class, they set about it with the kind of missionary zeal that many in today's secular world would regard with cool condescension. But no one should be smug about their efforts, for with virtually no government support, and in the face of overwhelming need, the Lady Managers and their sisters operating the handful of other child rescue agencies throughout the city, offered the only hope many children had of escaping disease, starvation and, all too often, death. Long before women won the right to vote and to hold public office, the Lady Managers established themselves as leaders in the field of child welfare. They maintained their presence throughout the foster care years until, in the early 1960s, the Agency transformed itself into Greater Toronto's primary home day care provider. But all through the years, the commitment to quality services for children and families remained unshakable.

Generations have passed since a homeless orphan named Tom had to scavenge for food amid the wharves and back alleys of a dirty colonial town. And yet a bond exists between him and well-loved, well-fed Jordan Richards. That bond is a venerable agency that celebrates its 150th anniversary in 2001. In that time, it has been a sanctuary and, in a very real sense, a second home to thousands of orphan, foster, and child care children, whose lives have been and will continue to be profoundly changed for the good by the experience.

In each period of Family Day's history, the Agency, always in touch with and responsive to community needs, devised and delivered programs to children and their families in advance of government financial support or regulation. Indeed, in the initial stages, the programs they provided invariably met with official indifference or outright resistance. In time, and given enough advocacy and prodding in the media, various levels of government would yield to public pressure and support a particular initiative.

As Family Day begins its 151st year, it is once again faced with the challenge of re-inventing itself. It faces the challenge of transforming government perception yet again by encouraging legislators to recognize the need for a new way of thinking about child care. Instead of thinking about child care as a welfare service, current research suggests that it should be regarded as a child development and family support service offering children valuable care and educational experiences and supporting parents in their efforts to raise their children. Quality home child care also contributes to the community by freeing parents to work, by enabling them to become reliable workers who are able to provide financially for their families, pay taxes and otherwise contribute to the economy.

As we have seen in these pages, the history of the agency has exemplified the vital leadership role that voluntary agencies play in our society by continuing to evolve, to initiate new programs to respond to changing social needs and new thinking about children and families. And, while there has been progress in many areas over the last century and a half, the need for continuing stewardship remains. As in earlier times, it is not clear where the new work of developing an alternative framework for family child care will lead, nor how it will become more integrated with other agency and community programs. What is clear, however, is that the guiding principles of high quality, of continuing care and concern for children and families' well-being will remain intact and be reflected in whatever programs and services are developed. There is also little doubt that the next 150 years of Family Day will be as challenging as the last.

150 Years of Caring for Children and Families

The United Way of Greater Toronto

Family Day Care Services has been a member agency of the United Way of Greater Toronto since the United Way's inception here in 1956. Over the past 45 years, the United Way has contributed more than six million dollars in support of Family Day's Toronto Home Child Care Program. These funds have allowed Family Day to provide a higher level of support to low-income families with children in care.

In addition to this annual support, the United Way has provided special funding for a number of projects initiated by Family Day, including a home child care pilot project in East York and a community resource centre in Flemingdon Park.

Family Day Care Services

Community Chest of Greater Toronto

From 1945 to 1955, Protestant Childrens' Homes received financial support from The Community Chest of Greater Toronto's annual Red Feather Campaign. The Agency received a total of $683,880 during this eleven-year period in support of its foster care program for children.

Federation For Community Service of Toronto

The Federation For Community Service of Toronto initially provided funding for both The Protestant Orphans' Home and The Girls' Home from 1921 to 1925. In 1926, the Federation assisted in bringing about the amalgamation of the two organizations, then provided financial support for The Protestant Children's Home until 1944 with an average annual gift of $22,000.

Extract From the Federation For Community Service of Toronto's 1926 Annual Report:

"The Protestant Orphans' Home and "The Girls' Home," two of our oldest and most honored member organizations, have, after mature consideration secured enabling legislation, amalgamated their work and resources and will in future, operate as one organization. This is an indication that the institutional type of care for children has diminished, for in former years both these organizations were taxed to capacity. Now the institutional population is relatively small and increasing numbers will receive supervised care in well selected family boarding homes. It is gratifying to be able to report that this difficult end was achieved by these Boards in a fine spirit of devotion to what they conceived to be the best present day standards of social work for dependent children. The new organization known as "The Protestant Children's Home" will have the congratulations and the good wishes of its many friends. In giving the community long years of faithful service as separate Institutions and now in merging their resources, traditions, affections and interests in one organization which will operate along lines of service approved by social workers today, these Boards have placed the community under a lasting debt of gratitude, and in addition have given Toronto an example of how a difficult adjustment may be made to meet new conditions and standards of work."

Community Partners

OSLER, HOSKIN & HARCOURT

Osler, Hoskin & Harcourt has been a leading community partner with our Agency for more than a century. This renowned Toronto-based law firm has supported us over the years with in-kind contributions of legal services. In addition, since the late 19th century, many of the firm's senior staff and their family members have served on our Board of Directors, and made generous financial contributions to support us.

PriceWaterhouseCoopers

PriceWaterhouseCoopers, an international professional services firm, has been helping Family Day Care Services for more than three decades with in-kind contributions of financial planning services. As well, a number of the firm's staff members have provided leadership on our Board of Directors and given personal donations to support our child care programs.

These community partners are to be commended for providing continuous support and leadership to our Agency, and for their long-standing dedication to enhancing child care services in the Province of Ontario.

For the Children

... and their future.

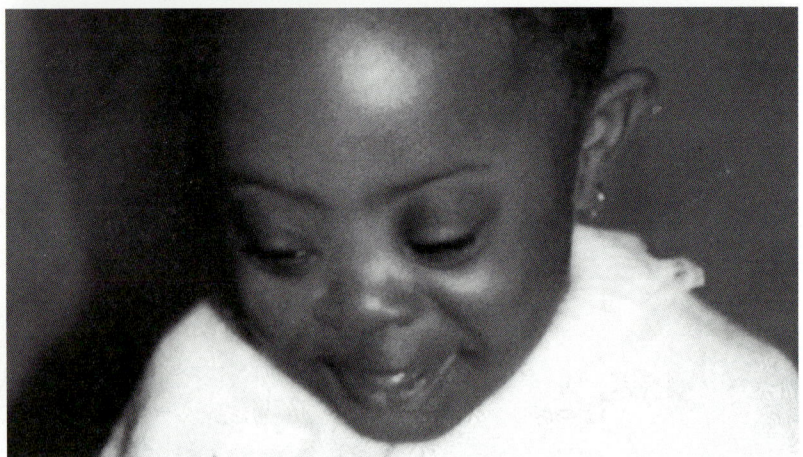

Family Day Care Services

150 Years of Caring for Children and Families

Family Day Care Services

150 Years of Caring for Children and Families

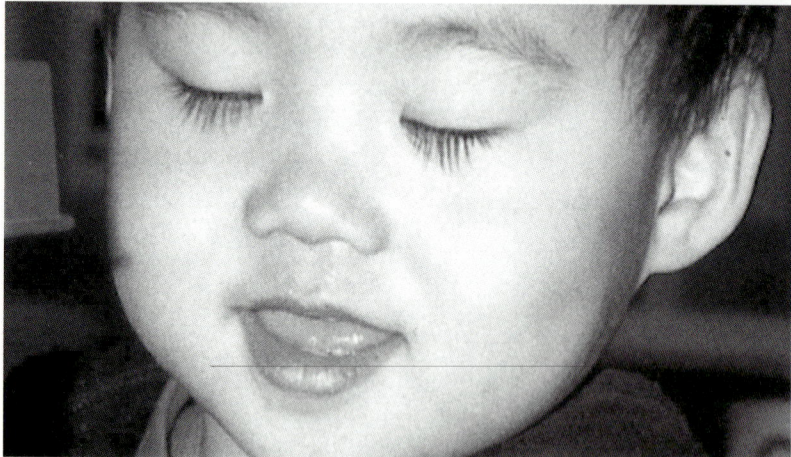

Family Day Care Services

150 Years of Caring for Children and Families

Family Day Care Services

150th anniversary
Family Day

Photo Album

Thanks for the Memories
as we Celebrate
50 years at
380
Sherbourne
Street
Family Day

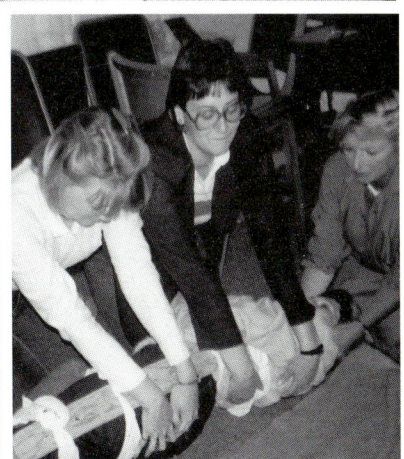

150 Years of Caring for Children and Families

Family Day Care Services

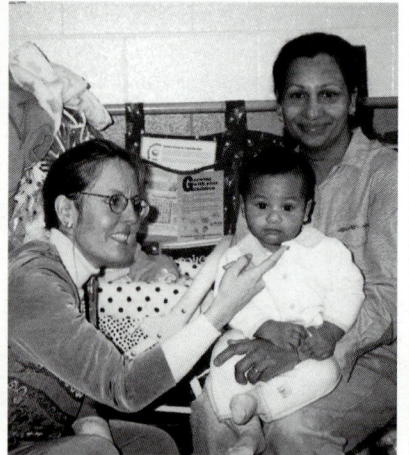

150 Years of Caring for Children and Families

Family Day Care Services

150 Years of Caring for Children and Families

175

Family Day Care Services

150 Years of Caring for Children and Families

Photo Credits

Page	Photo	Credit
2	Toronto Canada West (1854) sketch	Artist: Whitefield, Edwin by permission of City of Toronto Art Collection, Culture Division
3	SC1, Item 31	City of Toronto Archives
6	St Lawrence Hall sketch	Artist: Hornyansky, N. by permission of City of Toronto Art Collection, Culture Division
9	St. James Cathedral sketch	Artist: Hornyansky, N. by permission of City of Toronto Art Collection, Culture Division
14	T33064 Bishop Strachan	Metro Toronto Reference Library
16	SC 244, Item 130	City of Toronto Archives
17	SC 1, Item 16	City of Toronto Archives
18	SC 1, Item 36	City of Toronto Archives
26	T30826 Robert Baldwin	Metro Toronto Reference Library
28	House of Providence	Archives of the Roman Catholic Archdiocese of Toronto
31	John Joseph Kelso	by permission of Children's Aid Society of Toronto
33	Motherless	by permission of the Glasgow Art Gallery
36	SC 1, Item 14	City of Toronto Archives
39	SC 244, Item 21A	City of Toronto Archives
42	Item 151027	City of Toronto Archives. Globe & Mail Collection
44	SC 244, Item 132A	City of Toronto Archives
56	T15182 John Gooderham Sr.	Metro Toronto Reference Library, J. Ross Roberston Collection
57	Gooderham & Worts Factory sketch	Artist: Hider, A. H. by permission of City of Toronto Art Collection, Culture Division
58	SC 244, Item 8032	City of Toronto Archives
60	SC 244, Item 8028	City of Toronto Archives
79	RG 28, Item 67	City of Toronto Archives
80	RG 28, Item 57	City of Toronto Archives
82	Item 81679	City of Toronto Archives. Globe & Mail Collection
82	Item 81678	City of Toronto Archives. Globe & Mail Collection
84	Item 81635	City of Toronto Archives. Globe & Mail Collection
85	Item 81644	City of Toronto Archives. Globe & Mail Collection
86	Item 81643	City of Toronto Archives. Globe & Mail Collection
92	Item 81670	City of Toronto Archives. Globe & Mail Collection
98	Item 148688	City of Toronto Archives. Globe & Mail Collection
99	Mr. and Mrs. Jack Frisby	Toronto Daily Star, Friday May 9, 1958; Star Photo by Ted Dinsmore
102	Warren Reynolds holds six month old Inuit boy	Reprinted with permission - Courtesy of The Toronto Star Syndicate

All remaining photos are from the Family Day Care Services Archives